STEAM IN
WARTIME BRITAIN

Three groups are represented in this view of Manchester London Road station taken in April 1940, some seven months after the outbreak of hostilities. The arriving LMS train from Birmingham is headed by 'Patriot' class 6P5F 4–6–0 locomotive No. 5502 *Royal Naval Division*. Behind the water tank are GWR coaches and beyond these can be seen LNER stock. The picture was taken from a concealed spot on the lattice girder foot-bridge and the only confirmation of the war lies in the boxed gas masks slung from the shoulders of the young spotters on the adjacent platform.

STEAM IN WARTIME BRITAIN

KENNETH OLDHAM

ALAN SUTTON

First published in the United Kingdom in 1993 by
Alan Sutton Publishing Ltd · Phoenix Mill · Stroud · Gloucestershire

First published in the United States of America in 1993 by
Alan Sutton Publishing Inc · 83 Washington Street · Dover · NH 03820

Reprinted 1993, 1994

British Library Cataloguing in Publication Data

Oldham, Kenneth
Steam in Wartime Britain
I. Title
625.2610941

ISBN 0-7509-0325-2

Library of Congress Cataloging in Publication Data

Oldham, Kenneth.
Steam in Wartime Britain: LMS and LNER/Kenneth Oldham.
p.cm.
Includes bibliographical references.
ISBN 0-7509-0325-2: $33.00
1. Railroads – Great Britain – History. 2. World War. 1939–1945 –
Transportation. I. Title
TF57.048 1993
625.2'61'094109044 – dc20   92–45036
                                                            CIP

*Jacket photographs: front: from a painting by Eric Oldham; back: class D2 4–4–0 No. 4390 from a
photograph by Kenneth Oldham. Endpapers: front: No. 6126, Royal Army Service Corps,
departing from Manchester London Road on a suburban stopping train to Crewe; back: class VI
No. 2899 steams through Princes Street Gardens.*

Typeset in 10/12 Palatino.
Typesetting and origination by
Alan Sutton Publishing Limited.
Printed in Great Britain by
Butler & Tanner Ltd, Frome and London.

CONTENTS

INTRODUCTION   vii

CHAPTER 1   HALCYON DAYS OF THE THIRTIES   1

CHAPTER 2   THE RAILWAYS IN WARTIME BRITAIN   17

             THE MANCHESTER AREA, 1940 to 1941, LMS and LNER   26

             THE WOODHEAD LINE, 1940 to 1942, LNER   43

CHAPTER 3   EXPLOITS OF A MOBILE PHOTOGRAPHER   91

             THE EAST AND WEST COAST MAIN LINE   98
             (a)   THE WEST COAST MAIN LINE IN CHESHIRE
                    AND SOUTH LANCASHIRE, 1941, LMS
             (b)   THE MAIN LINE AT WINWICK QUAY,
                    NORTH OF WARRINGTON, APRIL/MAY, 1941, LMSR
             (c)   THE EAST COAST MAIN LINE SOUTH OF
                    DONCASTER, 1941, LNER

             THE GRAND TOUR, 6 – 14 JUNE 1941   131
             (a)   THE EAST COAST MAIN LINE, LNER
             (b)   THE WEST COAST MAIN LINE, LMS

             A FINAL GLIMPSE OF THE LNER, 1941 TO 1943   163

A PROPHECY FULFILLED?   167

BIBLIOGRAPHY   168

An absolutely forbidden subject – the incredible cross-over junctions and signal gantry at the north end of Newcastle Central station viewed from the castle keep through a narrow slit in the stone staircase walls formerly used by archers in defensive position. This gave concealment for an opportunity too good to be missed – the departure of the wartime equivalent of the Down 'Flying Scotsman' with A4 'Pacific' No. 4491 *Commonwealth of Australia* at the head. The photograph was taken while on leave in September 1943.

INTRODUCTION

A photographic record depicting the railways during the early war years would be incomplete if it did not include some reference to the period immediately preceding the outbreak of hostilities. The first short chapter conveys the atmosphere of that time, when east and west coast main lines vied with each other in the exciting era of the streamlined trains.

Although this work explores the northern part of these two main lines, a major section is devoted to the north-west and in particular to the scenic line of the former Great Central route from Manchester to Woodhead. Although Manchester London Road station and Longsight shed of the LMS are fully portrayed, wartime regulations caused a diversion away from the stations to more remote areas where clandestine photographic activities could be undertaken with the minimum risk. Many of the lineside vantage points were accessible only on foot. The early fall of France and the grave threat of invasion during September 1940 created a very wary outlook among the population, not eased by the ensuing blitz and degeneration of the war situation as one adversity followed another until, finally, the tide turned in our favour in November 1942. The Germans' use of the 'Fifth Column' in countries that fell to their onslaught heightened fears and resulted in a flood of published and broadcast warnings. 'Careless talk costs lives' and 'Walls have ears' were among many such cautions. Those who took notes or made observations at railway stations suddenly became objects of suspicion. Anyone seen using a camera in the neighbourhood of a railway was certainly very liable to suspicion, and it was against this background that the photographs which illustrate this work were taken. The occasional lineside pursuit and one brief arrest might be considered as a fair exchange for what is now a permanent record of that unique period of our railway history and one which has not been published before – that of railways in wartime Britain from 1939 to 1943.

The locations are largely scenic, the photographs aiming to produce aesthetic images of the steam locomotives at work. A few of the prints reproduce the wartime 'grain' as the choice and availability of film stock was variable, but this does not detract from the atmospheric quality and historic value of the pictures. A wide range of locomotives is depicted from the veterans that survived because their extended lifespan helped in the wartime emergency to the mightiest of the steam locomotives of the day which, in joining the national task of working for victory, undertook even the most mundane tasks.

The commentary linked to the photographs offers a wealth of information way beyond mechanical detail and provides an insight into the general background of the railways in wartime. The lack of maintenance that led to some deterioration in both performance and appearance was gradual in its effect, but this work covers the period between 1939 and

1943 before the worst of that inescapable conclusion, and it reflects great merit on the railway staff who worked under such extraordinary conditions during that period and served the nation so well.

April 1993   Kenneth Oldham

CHAPTER ONE

HALCYON DAYS OF THE THIRTIES

A gradual but accumulative series of events relating to the sheer enjoyment of the railway scene triggered off a lifelong interest that developed into something of an obsession – a passionate desire to capture on film the splendour of steam engines in action.

If there was an initiation, it was the unforgettable sight and sound of an LNER express early in 1931 when I was taken by my grandfather to watch the trains at Godley on the former Great Central line from Manchester over Woodhead to Sheffield. The splendour of the glistening apple green locomotive rocking wildly above the flashing rods and pistons, the shrill whistle echoing across the hills until overtaken by the relentless staccato beat of the exhaust, the final swish and synchronized wheel-beat as the mirror-finish teak coaches swept by; all made an indelible impression upon my young mind. I knew nothing of 'Gorton Tank' where the cleaners had put such a sparkling finish to the crack express, but I had reached the age where I could read well enough to decipher the engine name, *Raby Castle*, and to read aloud the words on the white destination boards affixed to the highly polished teak coaches – 'Continental Boat Express' and 'Liverpool–Harwich' among a host of other places. I could hardly wait to get home to tell my elder brother, Eric, what I had seen. He advised me that the engine was a 'Sandringham' – another good name to add to my vocabulary. My requests at this early age to join him on his regular visits to the line were refused. 'You're always staggering about. It's too far for you,' he said. Only many years later did it become apparent that he had been preaching to a potential long distance walker!

Railways and tramways were already facing the strengthening challenge of road transport. Roads were being improved constantly and although up to the mid-thirties road vehicles were relatively few, their numbers unremittingly increased. Buses offered a good alternative choice for short distances and an appreciable quantity of goods was also transported by road, but the bulk of the population continued to travel by rail. 'It's quicker by rail', the posters exhorted as the competition became keener.

Early rail journeys included the occasional Sundays when Eric and I joined our father on his early morning excursions with the Hyde Fishing Club on trips from Hyde to Poynton, Macclesfield or Bollington. The imposing and airy canopy above the entrance to Hyde station was a total contrast to the large booking-hall which was forever dark and sombre in the gas-lit atmosphere. Echoing wooden stairs led to the near platform. We never had long to wait. After the initial warning from the station bell, a hoarse whistle heralded the immediate approach of the train which was invariably hauled by an old tank engine, an immaculate class F1 2–4–2 of Great Central origin.

The fishermen gathered up their bits and pieces as the train of six-wheeled coaches rumbled to a halt. Horizontal brass handles were firmly gripped and turned to open the doors as the anglers, in jocular and unhurried fashion, climbed aboard. Their awkward bundles were dumped onto the bench seats or jammed onto the racks above: extended bags that held their rods; other bags of varied shapes and sizes; and the large wicker baskets that served them later as seats. These held hooks, lines, reels, spinners and floats as well as the tins of maggots that would entice their prey, and an appropriate lunch and flask of tea to meet the fishermen's other needs. A few carried bait cans with 'live bait' and these were carefully placed on the floor.

As the small groups settled, doors slammed behind them and arms reached out from the open windows to turn each brass handle from the outer side to make them secure in the horizontal locked position. There were no internal catches on these doors. Leather straps hoisted the windows to a more acceptable level for the journey. At the rear of the train, porters hurriedly loaded baskets of homing pigeons into the guard's compartment for release by staff at some distant station at a carefully pre-determined time. After the porters had checked and confirmed the security of the doors, the guard signalled the driver with a long blast on his whistle as he held the green flag aloft. With a brief hoarse whistle from the engine and a very slow and methodic deep-throated puffing, the train moved off. The pace was always leisurely and every station, a halt.

Hyde Fishing Club on a competition outing await the arrival of the local stopping train at Newton station, *c.* 1928.

The journeys in the opposite direction, from Hyde to Manchester, bustled with potential shoppers going to town. As the train rumbled to a halt we jumped up and down on the platform to spot a compartment with a vacant window seat on the far side. There was a special bonus to be had from such a vantage point. The train passed alongside the former Great Central Gorton works where recently outshopped locomotives glistened in their pristine glory. Other columns of locomotives lined up at the nearby sheds or, best of all, queued by the coaling plant adjacent to the main line. Gleaming 'Sandringhams' vied with immaculate 'Directors' or with the impressive and varied 'B' class 4–6–0s of Robinson's design. Early in November you could count on seeing B3 No. 6165 *Valour*, the Great Central 'Memorial' engine, distinctive with its large shield shaped name-plates inscribed to the memory of employees who fell in the First World War. Just prior to Armistice Day, the locomotive received very special treatment with extra spit and polish for the Remembrance Day service always held at 11 a.m. on 11 November. It invariably headed the Manchester–Sheffield express as a gleaming tribute bearing token wreaths on each ornate name-plate and on the front. At Sheffield it took part in a special service of remembrance to commemorate the dead.

A transfer of allegiance took place shortly after passing Gorton as the window on the opposite side offered views of the LMSR main line on the final approach from Ardwick to the main terminus at Manchester London Road (now Manchester Piccadilly). On occasion we would catch the 'Director'- hauled Cleethorpes–Manchester express from Newton station and enjoy the fast journey with only a single stop (Guide Bridge) before the smooth glide into London Road station. On that final stretch our train often ran neck and neck with the Down 'Comet' express hauled by a 'Royal Scot' from Euston and due to arrive on the LMS side at around 3.20 p.m., the same time as the Cleethorpes express on the LNE.

Manchester London Road was in effect two stations side by side beneath a four-arched roof span supported by massive iron columns and strengthened by latticed girders. Two companies, the early Manchester Sheffield and Lincolnshire Railway and the London and North Western Railway, were separated by heavy iron railings, a Victorian 'Iron Curtain' from the days when competition was not only rife, but occasionally spilled into violence! When the MS&L Rly first allowed Great Northern trains to run from King's Cross to Manchester late in 1857 the LNWR opposed this development of a route that compared favourably with their own route from London in terms of distance, speed and comfort, and they arrested passengers who arrived at London Road station on Great Northern trains. This deterrent action ended somewhat abruptly after the apprehension of a lawyer and the matter was settled shortly afterwards by an agreement to share the traffic. The rivalry continued and as late as 1882 when the MS&L lit their side of the station by electricity, one of the first public buildings in Manchester to achieve this distinction, it was rumoured that Sir Edward Watkin, MS&L chairman at that time, directed that shades should be fitted to the lights to prevent illumination falling on the LNW's side. As a boy I remember great hoardings separating the two and was told that they were to 'prevent things being hurled from one side to the other'.

In the early thirties there was a friendly rivalry and the station offered a wealth of opportunities for the railway enthusiast. The ticket barriers for all the LNER platforms and for the LMS departure platforms were in line and to avoid confusion, the former company lettered its platforms A to D while the LMS numbered off consecutively from platform 1. As there were no barriers to the LMS arrival platforms, this allowed free access to the whole of that section of the station and the far ends of the platforms provided splendid vantage points to observe all comings and goings. A foot-bridge near this open end made it easy to transfer from one platform to another and if the LNER ticket cabin on the bridge was unstaffed, there was additional free access to the LNER platforms as well.

By 1934 my brother and I had both acquired new Coronet box cameras and with this basic equipment set out to record the Manchester to Sheffield old Great Central line at Hyde junction. A cutting provided an ideal viewpoint from which we recorded the passing of the Continental Boat express and the London Marylebone express, both hauled by 'Sandringhams', and the Cleethorpes express invariably hauled by a 'Director'. The moderately distant images did not appear too blurred on the small contact prints and they stimulated the appetite for more.

Few periods in our railway history compare with the exciting events during those years just prior to the Second World War when new records were attained with some frequency by the big engines of the rival east and west coast main lines. Scarcely a month passed without the newspapers acclaiming some memorable achievement: *Flying Scotsman's* 100 m.p.h.; *Papyrus* reaching 108 m.p.h.; and the thrilling climax of the streamlined trains on both routes initiated by *Silver Link*'s remarkable run with the 'Silver Jubilee', the snatching of the speed record by the 'Coronation Scot' of the LMS at 114 m.p.h. and the classic retrieval by *Mallard* of the LNER at 126 m.p.h.

We had never seen a 'Pacific' and in the spring of 1935 made the first of many visits to Doncaster for this very purpose. Sunday excursion trains, always hauled by an immaculate K3 2–6–0, were the means to this end. As juveniles we travelled at the half-fare rate of 1s. 9d. (about 9p) from Godley junction, arriving at Doncaster by the late morning.

We were astounded by the never-ending procession of trains which called at the platforms or hurtled past on the through lines. Only for a short spell in the mid-afternoon was there a lull. By the end of that hour, the heavy traffic had again built up. The bell in the signal-box indicated another express was due and the signal levers were pulled in sequence to activate the signals as one by one the Great Northern somersaults lunged into the 'off' position. A couple of minutes later, the train would appear.

We were spellbound, not only by Gresley's 'Pacifics' but by the whole extraordinary range of locomotives that paraded by. New 'Sandringhams', 'Directors' and Great Northern 'Atlantics' were marked off in our notebooks, but at Doncaster they were supported by a wide variety of both vintage and more recent examples of Great Northern and North Eastern design. 'Hunts' and 'Shires' were dwarfed by the massive Raven A2 'Pacifics' of Darlington origin. No. 2404 *City of Ripon* and No. 2400 *City of Newcastle* were both recorded on that first day, but it was the wealth of Gresley's magnificent 'Pacifics' that held the stage. Immaculate and with white hinges on the smokebox doors, they had an air of distinction that set them apart from the rest and they created their own enduring impression. The previous month, *Cock o' the North* was a regular visitor.

Not until the spring of 1936 were we able to make our second trip to Doncaster. The varied and unceasing cavalcade, for that it was, matched exactly our previous visit, but at ten minutes to four on that Sunday afternoon the calm was broken by a most melodious chime whistle. Shortly afterwards an unforgettable vision of silver-grey came into view as we witnessed our first A4 'Pacific' sweeping round the curve beyond St James's Bridge, its inverted pear-shaped front glistening in the sun. With further long and superbly melodious warning chimes, Gresley's masterpiece powered the express through the station in elegant and effortless splendour. The silver bands that embellished the boiler and the silver fox affixed beneath the painted name *Silver Fox* gave an added spice to the pleasure of that memorable experience.

From that time on, whenever the 'ten-to-four' express was signalled on the through line, we knew that it would be an A4 'Pacific'. The only exception was a one-off when the train was hauled by an A1. However, the natural disappointment to the young minds that it was not a streamliner dissipated as soon as we recognized the number 4472 and the world renowned name, *Flying Scotsman* – our first viewing of this famous locomotive. Even then, it was followed within the hour by a Down stopping train for Newcastle hauled by No. 2509 *Silver Link* and the pleasure of seeing an A4 on each visit remained unbroken. The ten-to-four express, we later discovered, was a balancing turn for the 'Silver Jubilee' locomotive.

As the months progressed it seemed that every visit excelled the expectations based on previous visits. A new design emerged, the V2 2–6–2 class, and I was invited into the cab of the first of the class, 4771 *Green Arrow*, as it prepared for departure. A new batch of streamliners appeared, the first of which, No. 4482 *Golden Eagle*, was observed early in 1937 resplendent in the apple green livery that was for a short time to be standardized as befitting the highly polished teak coaches of the crack express trains. By July of that year the 'Coronation' made its debut. We glimpsed the coaches heading south as our Sunday special was held up at St James's Bridge on the approach to Doncaster station. The engine had already passed the short gap where the main line was visible from our train and we were unaware of the presence of a blue A4, but the colour scheme of the new streamlined train led to all sorts of speculation and the 'beaver tail' observation coach at the rear left no doubt that once again Gresley had excelled. We surmised later that the train was heading for Retford to the place where the official photographs of the train were taken before it came into service.

By 1938, there were four silver-grey A4s, seven with the Garter blue livery and an increasing number in apple green. As they approached at angles which gave a mainly frontal view, it was impossible to judge the colour which was eclipsed by brilliant reflections, all of which added to the joy of anticipation. Only as they neared was it possible to identify the livery. In the holiday season, even on Sundays, we observed as many as three A4s simultaneously on the Up arrival track – one in the platform and two others held by signals at the northern end of the station awaiting their turn to enter. The colours on one occasion exemplified the full range!

In the summer of that year a family holiday to Bridlington provided the opportunity to visit York and, with a 'runabout' ticket, Eric and I made two visits. We caught the 'Shire'-hauled 'Scarborough Flier' for a fast run to York and saw for the first time the many named expresses that ran on weekdays – the 'Flying Scotsman', the 'Silver Jubilee' and the 'Coronation' among them. We were ecstatic, but it was the 'crowning glory' of the LNER, the 'Coronation', that made the greatest impact. With the severe limitations that a box camera imposed, I positioned myself on a side platform to take a more distant shot as the 'Coronation' slowed for its three minute halt. Framed by a signal gantry and at a distance sufficient to encompass the whole train, a shutter speed of a mere 1/25th second managed for once to produce a satisfying and attractive image. A high-speed chase to change platforms within the allotted timespan enabled me to set up the camera for a time exposure within the arched splendour of the station. Without a tripod or support, the camera was held firmly on the platform for a four second exposure of the 'beaver tail'. The two pictures, taken by such primitive equipment and at the age of fourteen, are among my most treasured photographs.

There was just time to take in some of the splendour. The twin red tail lamps of the 'beaver tail' and its curved windows and outline emphasized its uniqueness. The whole train was appropriately coloured Garter blue to the waist with Marlborough blue above, and the sides of each coach were adorned with stainless steel lettering and embellishments including the name 'CORONATION'. By each open door were the train attendants, equally resplendent in their smart Garter blue uniforms adorned with white lapels and silver buttons. Pure white gloves and matching blue peaked caps with white cap bands completed the ensemble. The sheer beauty and extravagance of the internal decor was beyond anything that I had seen before (or have seen since): swivelling armchairs; 'Rexine' covered walls decorated with aluminium frets with an elaborate 'crown' motif; and the open and decorative partitions which separated the sections to provide free access without draughts or loss of privacy and so arranged that every passenger could enjoy a meal or refreshment without moving from his table seat. Two kitchens supplied the needs of the passengers. As I walked alongside, making my way to the engine, I allowed my hand to glide smoothly along the gleaming sides of the coaches in an almost sensual manner. The whole train was washed with 'Lux' after every journey. *Golden Eagle*, in Garter blue and with the deep wine-red wheels, was at the head of the train which left precisely on time after the brief three minute stop – one of the most vivid three minutes in the whole of my life!

Apart from those two sightings at York and the pre-inaugural glimpse of the train at Doncaster, I only saw it in normal service on two more occasions when, in 1939, I made two weekday visits to Doncaster. In these days of reduced services it is worth recording the high level of activity noted on a weekday in August 1939, less than a month before the outbreak of war and the demise of the prestigious streamlined trains.

Only those subjects which were photographed were noted, along with their times for future photographic sorties, but a great many more trains and locomotives were seen. My box camera, or more truthfully, the young photographer, had a fixation on the bigger engines and the list reflects this rather than the wide variety and great number of loco-motive classes to be seen at the time. This is further evidenced by an appended note con-firming that on the first visit twenty-one different A4s were seen and on the second visit the total (including 4–6–4 No. 10000) reached twenty-three different streamlined locomotives.

Trains photographed during a mid-week day in August 1939

Time	Subject
11.47	4499 *Sir Murrough Wilson* with the Up 'Silver Jubilee'
11.55	4798 with Up Leeds–London express
12.04	4496 *Golden Shuttle* with the Up 'West Riding Limited'
12.12	4903 *Peregrine* with the Up 'Scarborough Flier'
12.14	GN 'Atlantic' 4456 with the Hull portion of the Up 'Yorkshire Pullman'
12.16	2751 *Humorist* takes over the Up 'Yorkshire Pullman'
12.30	V2 No. 4818 *St Peter's School, York*
12.35	4490 *Empire of India* with the Down 'Flying Scotsman'
12.45	4469 *Sir Ralph Wedgewood* at speed
12.50	4495 *Golden Fleece* stops with a Down King's Cross–Bridlington express
13.04	2578 *Bayardo* with express
13.15	4476 *Royal Lancer* stops with Newcastle–King's Cross express
13.16	2551 *Prince Palatine* stops with the Harrogate–King's Cross express
13.25	4467 *Wild Swan* with the Down 'Scarborough Flier'
13.53	4470 *Great Northern* with the Down 'Queen of Scots'
14.23	4498 *Sir Nigel Gresley* with the Up 'Flying Scotsman'
14.26	London Tank 4610
14.30	*Blink Bonny* with stopping train

14.47	2582 *Sir Hugo* with Up express
14.57	4500 *Sir Ronald Matthews* with Up express at speed
15.40	4900 *Gannet* stops with Down express
15.50	V2 No. 4777
16.00	4462 *Great Snipe* stops with Down express
16.15	4494 *Osprey* with Down express
16.16	2510 *Quicksilver*
16.30	4468 *Mallard*
16.32	2555 *Centenary* with Up 'Queen of Scots'
17.26	V2 No. 4792
17.30	NER 4–4–2 No. 706 with express
18.00	4467 *Wild Swan* stops with Up express
18.07	4488 *Union of South Africa* with the Down 'Coronation'
18.15	K3 No. 203 with express from Leeds. Taken over by 'Pacific'
19.03	4901 *Capercaillie* with Up express
19.03	4902 *Seagull* stops with King's Cross–Newcastle express
19.20	2751 *Humorist* with Down 'Yorkshire Pullman'
19.40	4489 *Dominion of Canada* with the Down 'Silver Jubilee'

The second day visit shows some interesting variations including three of the original four silver-grey A4s in the new Garter blue livery:

Time	Subject
11.40	4489 *Dominion of Canada* with the Up 'Silver Jubilee'
12.05	4496 *Golden Shuttle* with the Up 'West Riding Limited'
12.10	4903 *Peregrine* with the Up 'Scarborough Flier'
12.15	4477 *Gay Crusader* stops with the Up 'Yorkshire Pullman'
12.40	4490 *Empire of India* with the Down 'Flying Scotsman'
12.45	2510 *Quicksilver*
12.55	2578 *Bayardo* with Down King's Cross–Edinburgh express
13.30	2744 *Grand Parade* with the Down 'Scarborough Flier'

During the afternoon (some times not recorded):

	4467 *Wild Swan* with stopping train
	4–6–4 No. 10000 with express
	4484 *Falcon* with the Up 'Flying Scotsman'
	2511 *Silver King* (a rare appearance south of Newcastle)
	2555 *Centenary* with the Up 'Queen of Scots'
18.08	4492 *Dominion of New Zealand* with the Down 'Coronation'
19.00	4901 *Capercaillie* at speed
19.40	2509 *Silver Link* with the Down 'Silver Jubilee'
20.20	4482 *Golden Eagle* with the Up 'Coronation'
20.35	4463 *Sparrow Hawk* stops with a Down express
20.52	4468 *Mallard* stops with a Down express

The utter failure of my attempt to record the scene in colour prompted the second of the day visits as compensation. The very slow film speed of Dufaycolor was way beyond the capabilities of a mere box camera except perhaps by the use of the time exposure.

Even then, the brief time exposure of *Mallard* at the platform yielded little more than a very dark image. The rest of the film was totally blank. The second visit was more successful and the added bonus of a later return train allowed me to see the Up 'Coronation' as well as the down. Looking back, the list of locomotives reads something like a 'Who's Who' of the LNER stud.

The increasing numbers of A4s and V2s led to a reallocation of some of the older A1 'Pacifics' to the former Great Central line and they replaced the 'Sandringhams' on the crack expresses from Manchester to London Marylebone. No. 2558 *Tracery* took over the London express in October 1938 and by early March 1939 it was supported by 4474 *Victor Wild* and 4478 *Hermit*. 4473 *Solario* and 2554 *Woolwinder* added their presence in May and August of that same year. It was the first regular use of 'Pacifics' on what was 'home ground'.

Until that time, Grand National Day had been the one and only occasion when a 'Pacific' could be seen as it hauled a pullman special to and from Aintree. We always made a pilgrimage to Godley junction around six in the evening to watch the return procession of race specials invariably led by the pullman with an immaculate 'Pacific' at its head, frequently 4475 *Flying Fox*. Gleaming cranks, gilt lettering and the name-plate reflected the gas lamps which glowed feebly from the darkness of the platform. Such weak illumination failed to match the lighted table lamps that shone from the windows as the pullman glided through. The non-stop joined the old Great Central route over Woodhead and thence to London. The following race specials were double headed and all stopped for water before the long climb ahead. Ex-Great Central 4–6–0s took pride of place and amid all the activity, including drawing up for the second engine to take water, the station staff had some lively exchanges with the kitchen car attendants with whom it seemed they had placed their bets!

From October 1938 visits to Manchester London Road were rewarded by the sight of A1 'Pacifics' on the LNER side and 'Royal Scots' on the LMSR (not until the war years did LMS 'Pacifics' visit this station on a regular basis). I decided to make time exposures to record the station interior and on one day was delighted to obtain pictures of No. 2558 *Tracery* about to depart on the one side and No. 6100 *Royal Scot*, complete with its American bell and the special name-plate on the smokebox door, at the buffer stops on the LMS side. The enormous buffers provided a very firm base for the four second exposure with the box camera.

The west coast main line was a further attraction. On periodic visits to Warrington we saw the 'Coronation Scot', the 'Royal Scot' and many other crack trains of the day and were much impressed. The blurred images on our photographic records of the visits confirmed not only the element of speed, but the very great need for better equipment in the camera line.

My enthusiasm for the railways attracted the friendship of Raymond Fazakerley, the son of the station-master at Godley junction whose lineside station-master's house became a second home. At Hyde Grammar School which we attended, the sports field was alongside the track. I thoroughly enjoyed the games afternoons but not for the reasons intended by the education authority. As the goal-posts of the lower pitch were within yards of the railway boundary fence, it was not unusual to find me perched there when playing full back. If a train distracted me while I was defending goal, a lynching party sometimes formed. Mr Cousins, the games master during my final year, 1939/40, must have despaired at my lack of commitment on the field, but he was himself a rail enthusiast and I was delighted when he gave me permission to visit the signal-box at Newton on a regular basis during games. The box lay just beyond the roadbridge by the playing field and I had already established a friendship with the signalman, Mr Eccles, who allowed me to operate the signal levers under his supervision. The small desk-top pneumatic levers resisted the initial pull as the safety mechanisms cleared the action, thus allowing the second stage of the pull to activate the signal or point. I argued that this could be considered a form of exercise and to Mr Cousins, no doubt tormented by my football antics and the lynching episodes, this must have seemed a most appropriate response!

I considered myself most fortunate to have experienced that exciting era during my childhood and to have experienced the thrill of the streamlined trains which were such a highlight until the war. The only disappointing factor was the inability to capture the high speed moments with such totally inadequate camera equipment.

This was to change, however. A new camera, the 'Purma Special', made entirely of new plastic materials apart from the lens and shutter, was launched on the market. With a fixed focus lens from ten feet to infinity and f6.3 aperture, a focal plane shutter offering 1/25, 1/150 and 1/450 second, and an advertised cost of £2 10s. (£2.50) it was ideal; the perfect camera for railway photographers of limited means, and an enthusiastic school-boy fitted that category exactly!

During the months that I saved to purchase the new camera, I perused much advertising literature to calculate the new opportunities that would unfold with an f6.3 lens and such a shutter. However, before I could pay for the instrument and put it to good use, the streamlined trains were all taken out of service. It was the end of August 1939. War was imminent. Far more than the camera was going to change and by the time that I was able to purchase my 'Purma', the War Office had issued an order which placed a clear ban on railway photography.

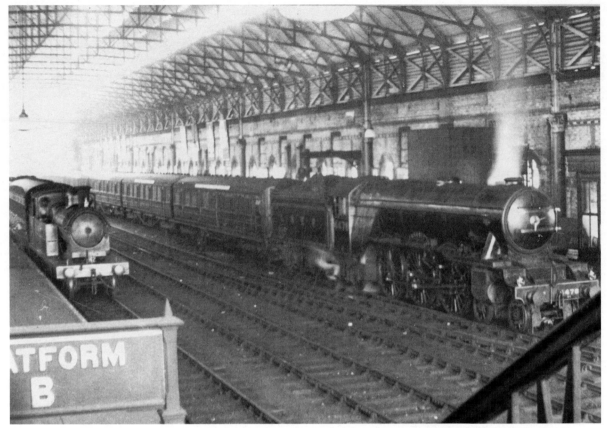

The LNER section of Manchester London Road station comprised only three platforms identified by the letters 'A', 'B' and 'C' respectively. The use of letters to identify platforms was unique to the former Great Central and was retained after the groupings. It avoided the confusion that might have arisen at the platform entrance barriers which the LMS numbered consecutively from platform 1 in their section.

This box camera time exposure was taken from the steps of the foot-bridge by platform 'B' shortly before the 2.20 p.m. departure of the Up London Marylebone express. The over-arm signal that controlled departures from platform 'A' can be seen behind the tender of Class A1 'Pacific' No. 4478 *Hermit*. The suburban train at platform 'B' is headed by Class C13 4–4–2T No. 5050 built by the Great Central Railway at Gorton in December 1904.

Platform 'A' was normally, although not exclusively, reserved for the main express trains, whereas platforms 'B' and 'C' were the normal departure platforms for Glossop, Hayfield, Macclesfield and other relatively local services. The two centre tracks of the four roads that separated platforms 'A' and 'B' were used for storage to reduce empty stock movements to and from the carriage sidings at Ardwick. Only a single road existed between platforms 'B' and 'C' and this served both platforms.

A1 'Pacific' No. 2558 *Tracery* was allocated to Gorton in October 1938 and was joined by others of the class in 1939. This platform level box camera time exposure reveals the magnificent splendour of the locomotive front end prior to the locomotive's departure on the 2.20 p.m. Up Marylebone express in the summer of 1939. The corniced pillar to the left of the engine marks the limit of the LNER (former Great Central Railway) section of Manchester London Road station. Beyond it lies the LMS terminus.

The immaculate state of the LNER A1 'Pacific' No. 4478 *Hermit*, matched by a mirror finish on the highly polished teak coaches, was the normal standard for the 2.20 p.m. Manchester–London Marylebone express. At Gorton Tank where the 'Pacific' was allocated, the engine was attended to by two senior cleaners known as 'Bogie Cleaners', each doing one side of the engine.

This time exposure from the central foot-bridge in the summer of 1938 shows York station at a time when the Penzance–Newcastle through train is having its water supply topped up through the roof panels. LNER Class D49 'Hunt' Class No. 269 *The Cleveland* has brought a stopping train from Hull into platform 4 south on what is normally the Down main platform. A train of empty stock occupies the Down 'through' line. The rear coach of this train, a six-wheeled vintage third class carriage with a guard's compartment, contrasts with the early bogie coach behind the 'Hunt' and the more modern GWR stock on the right. The 'ghost' on platform 4 is a person who moved away during the brief time exposure.

LMS locomotive No. 6100 *The Royal Scot,* bearing the unique smokebox name-plate and the bell presented on its American tour, was photographed at the buffer stops by the arrival platform 5 on the LMS side of Manchester London Road within the same half-hour as the photograph on page 11 depicting *Tracery* on the LNER.

LMS 'Royal Scot' No. 6101 *Royal Scots Grey* shortly after its arrival with 'The Comet' on platform 4 at Manchester London Road station. The headcode had been replaced by a single rear lamp as it was the normal practice for the locomotive to back out with the train when the pilot tank engine signalled the move from the far end of the platform. The express locomotive would then make its way to Longsight shed. 'The Comet' from London Euston on the LMS and the express from Cleethorpes on the LNE rivalled each other. They shared an arrival time of 3.20 p.m. and would often run neck and neck on the final stretch from Ardwick into Manchester London Road station.

The massive buffer stops at Manchester London Road station provided a very stable base for this box camera time exposure of LMS 'Patriot' Class 6P5F 4–6–0 No. 5521 *Rhyl* after its arrival on a train from Birmingham.

LMS 'Royal Scot' Class 7P 4–6–0 No. 6165 *The Ranger (12th London Regt)* awaits the departure time at Manchester London Road station at the head of a London Euston express. The steps to the left of the engine led from the platform end to the foot-bridge which gave access to all the tracks including those on the LNER.

The problem of the slow shutter speed of 1/25 second on the box camera was to some extent compensated by this more distant shot of the Down 'Coronation' hauled by A4 No. 4482 *Golden Eagle* as it slowed gently for its three minute stop at York. The whole train was appropriately coloured Garter blue to the waist and Marlborough blue above, and the sides of each coach were adorned with stainless steel lettering and embellishments including the name 'CORONATION'. Matching rubber sheeting between the coaches and the lower skirting gave an unbroken appearance along the full length of the train, and the splendour was matched by the Garter blue locomotive with its wine-red wheels. The massive signal gantries were a feature of the approach to York station and one such forms the balancing frame to this picture.

The magnificence of the 'beaver tail' observation coach of the 'Coronation' is captured in this classic photograph taken in July 1938 at York station. To a fourteen-year-old photographer without a tripod, the platform provided the required firm base on which to hold the box camera for the time exposure that produced this unusual angle. The twin red tail lamps were a feature of this unique express and the immaculate exterior finish never varied as the whole train was washed down with 'Lux' after every journey. It was equalled by the splendour of its internal decor and by the train attendants, resplendent in their Garter blue uniforms adorned with pristine white lapels and highly polished silver buttons. Pure white gloves and matching blue peaked caps with white cap bands completed the ensemble. The train was withdrawn from service on the outbreak of the Second World War and was never reinstated.

CHAPTER TWO

THE RAILWAYS IN WARTIME BRITAIN

The final runs of the streamlined trains on Thursday 31 August 1939 marked the end of that memorable era on the railways. Although the trains were stored safely throughout the war, the splendour of the late thirties was never regained.

On the Sunday morning of 3 September the nation listened intently as Mr Chamberlain's announcement followed the eleven o'clock striking of Big Ben, confirming the worst with quietly chilling words: '. . . I have to tell you now, that no such undertaking has been received, and that consequently, this country is at war with Germany.'

The strange feeling of relief that at last a firm decision had been taken was tempered by the dreadful memories of the First World War by the older generation and the natural tinge of excitement in the younger generation who pondered on the future course of events. Blackout conditions were immediately imposed and gas masks had to be carried at all times, by children and adults alike. The threat of immediate attack by air in one form or another was a reality that had to be faced and was emphasized when the warning sirens wailed early one night during the first week. We took shelter in the cellar and shortly afterwards the 'all clear' sounded. It had been a false alarm. Very little happened after that. It was the period of 'phoney' war and a sense of unreality pervaded despite the changes that were already underway.

On 1 September, two days before the war began, the Minister of Transport made an order under the Emergency Powers (Defence) Act 1939, taking control of the four British main line railways and the London Passenger Transport Board – and their joint committees. The minister appointed the Railway Executive Committee to give directions under the order. Passenger train services were considerably reduced as from 11 September.

Drivers, firemen and guards were supplied with special gas masks and steel helmets and all tender engines were fitted with tarpaulin screens to cover the space between cab and tender, preventing glare from open firebox doors on locomotives being observed from the air during the blackout hours. The October *Railway Magazine* commented: 'Anyone with experience of night flying realises with what comparative ease a main line railway may be recognised by the distinctive passage of the firebox glare along the track' and followed with a quote: 'Indeed it is nearly thirty years since Mr Claude Graham-

White demonstrated the possibilities of direction finding by locomotive light on his memorable night flight between London and Manchester.' The shielding of the firebox light was sensible but to suggest that a modern aircraft would be able to recognize a particular main line or the direction a line followed from such a brief encounter was surely stretching the imagination too far. However, the blackout was an essential precaution in those days before advanced navigation techniques. The hooding of electric signal lamps and the dimming (blue electric bulb) or shading of station lamps to allow only a restricted beam to shine downwards onto the platform, were among the precautions. The compulsory drawing of blinds within the coaches, which were initially only provided with dim blue light illumination, was among the other measures taken. As a further precaution the railway companies had prepared emergency headquarters outside the central London area, correctly judging the region to be at risk. For their operating staff who, of necessity, remained at their posts, they provided protective shelters.

One measure which brought some pleasure to the rail enthusiast was that locomotives of non-standard types which were serviceable, but which would otherwise have been scrapped, were preserved to ensure an adequate supply of engines to meet the requirements of any emergency that might arise, and the first of which was already underway.

Detailed arrangements for the rapid movement of some four million people from the threatened urban and industrial regions to relatively 'safe' areas had been prepared months before the outbreak of war. The essential timetables had been printed and stored to enable the swift evacuation of children and mothers to over twelve hundred stations near to their eventual destinations. The distribution by rail of emergency food supplies for the evacuated population was included within the timetabled operations. An advance warning poster announcing the arrangements for the evacuation was displayed at stations from 31 August, the details of which are given below:

Railway Passenger Services During Evacuation

The Main Line Railways announce that during Evacuation, alterations in the existing passenger services will be necessary, and the public are requested to limit their train travel to essential journeys.

London Suburban Services – Before 8 a.m. and after 5.30 p.m. services will be as near as possible normal. Between 8 a.m. and 5.30 p.m. skeleton services only will operate.

Provincial Suburban Services – During the hours of evacuation, skeleton services only will operate.

Main Line Services – The Railways expect to maintain Main Line services but no guarantee can be given as extensive alterations *to existing* timetables may have to be made without notice.

Despite the modifications, suburban travellers experienced very little inconvenience and although the streamlined trains and a few crack expresses had been cancelled, a relatively good main line service was maintained. By 11 September most expresses had been drastically curtailed and decelerated. Excursion and reduced fare facilities (except monthly return, week-end and workmen's tickets) were discontinued. It was no longer possible to book seats or to enjoy restaurant or buffet car facilities in general, but by 18 September the Southern Railway had put back into service a number of pullman buffet and pantry cars. On other railways, lengthy stops were made at important stations to allow passengers to obtain refreshments as had been the practice during an earlier period of railway history. By mid-October conditions improved and the restaurant car facilities were restored on a limited scale.

Further instructions were displayed concerning the action to be taken (or not to be taken) by passengers during an air raid:

1. Do not leave the train if it stops away from a station unless requested by the guard to do so. You are safer where you are.
2. Pull the blinds down on both sides day and night as a protection against flying glass.
3. If room is available, lie down on the floor.

The initial rail traffic had been considerable. Not only had the evacuation of some four million people proceeded according to plan but many other emergency arrangements were satisfactorily concluded. By the end of September 1,303,401 steel air-raid shelters capable of accommodating eight million persons had been delivered for free distribution in London alone. Shelters were placed at strategic points for the use of railway signalmen and the vital materials for repairs (sleepers, bridge girders, rails, electrical equipment and locomotive spare parts) were delivered to strategic sites to be available for immediate use in the anticipated emergencies. On top of this, other rail services for goods and for daily commuters ran almost normally despite the problems of blackout as the dark winter nights approached. At Euston station the blackout of the vast skylight roof was so effective that artificial lighting was required throughout the day. Military guards were posted at all important stations and bridges in London and elsewhere.

The *Railway Magazine* reminded its readers that many articles and comments of the type that had previously appeared in its pages would automatically come under a ban 'if there should be a possibility of their being useful to the enemy'. Correspondents were asked to refrain from asking questions in connection with such matters!

RESTRICTIONS ON PHOTOGRAPHY

Important restrictions on photography were contained in an order made by the War Office and announced by the Minister of Information on 11 September:

A permit must be granted before a person can photograph, sketch, plan or make any other representation of any of a lengthy list of objects, mainly of direct military import including any vessel or vehicle engaged in the transport of supplies or personnel; assembly of persons for transport or evacuation; roads or railways exclusively connected with works of defence. The photographic restrictions also apply to any object damaged by enemy action or as a result of any steps taken to repel enemy action.

The railway companies notified holders of photographic permits that, in consequence of the outbreak of war, it was no longer possible to grant facilities for taking photographs on railway premises and existing holders of permits were requested to return them.

Despite these restrictions and the further limitations concerning not only what could be published but also the amount of paper that could be supplied to publishers, it was surprising to find that in December 1939 a new railway publication, *Railways*, appeared on the station bookstalls. Both periodicals mentioned that, owing to war restrictions, the copies could only be supplied to newsagents on a non-returnable basis and to ensure receipt of a copy it would be necessary to place a standing order with the local newsagent.

Even more remarkable was an opening editorial in the first copy of the new magazine, which offered an open competition 'to encourage readers to produce better photographs'. They added a note of caution: 'We realise that during the war period railway photography is going to be very strictly limited, and we must advise readers against taking any photographs on railway property unless they have special permission to do so. Pre-war photos will be just as welcome as any other.'

The new magazine used good quality art paper and maintained a high standard of layout but with the limited supply of paper it restricted the publication to once every two months. By March 1940 it had become a monthly publication and was advertising that the first number had sold out and a reprint was being authorized to meet requests. The censor had evidently given advice concerning the illustration captions as the new magazine stated that 'where we consider it advisable we shall refrain from giving place-names in the descriptions of our illustrations.'

There was an almost amateurish approach to some aspects of what could or could not be done concerning railways. Despite the curtailing of excursion trains at the outbreak of the war, on the Thursday after Christmas, 1939, a special Cheltenham Races excursion ran from Paddington although the meeting had been declared 'off'. The train was halted at Slough and turned back to Paddington where the passengers received their fares back in full!

Another new regulation was devised to foil the enemy strategy whereby their planes might swoop low to read station names and thus be guided to their targets. Stations exhibiting large destination name boards were required to paint the letters out in dark grey to prevent such recognition from the air. They were equally difficult to read from the train and impossible in the blackout. This obsession about railways being a dominant aspect of air navigation must have been devised by the 'Armchair Brigade' who had little experience of such matters. Perhaps they based their conclusions from episodes in 'Biggles', for no self-respecting air navigator would have considered such an option when a much clearer image was printed on his navigation map that detailed the route to the target. However, the German bomber crews did not rely on maps. They used what was at the time an advanced radio beam system to guide them and a series of crossing radio beams to indicate the proximity of the target and the actual point at which to release their bombs.

Such peculiarities should not detract from the true effectiveness of the pre-war planning. During the First World War it was not until the spring of 1918, three-and-a-half years after the war had begun, that the final stage of deceleration and reduction of British train services was reached. In 1939 the changes to the full summer service, more drastic than in the latter part of 1918, were made almost overnight. In addition to the very serious cuts in the number of timetabled passenger trains, start to stop speeds were, in general, limited to 45 m.p.h. and maximum speeds were not expected to exceed 60 m.p.h. The average Midland time from St Pancras to Manchester Central was six hours and the entire former Great Central line from Marylebone to Sheffield and Manchester London Road initially reduced the major express through trains to one each way, leaving London or Manchester at 10 a.m. and calling at all principal stations, a journey of some six hours which was well over an hour longer than the best 1918 times. A further train ran at night.

After the massive transport demands of September, an unexpected result of the ensuing restrictions on travel was activated. Due to the reductions in train services, a considerably increased number of cleaners was available at the locomotive sheds. Engines whose colours and even numbers had been barely visible for some time through the heavy deposits of grime, were restored to a resplendent condition. Camden shed on the LMSR was reported as having a fine selection of shining 'Pacifics', 'Royal Scots' and other locomotives while the LNER again displayed the streamliners in their rightful shade of blue that had tended to be concealed by oil and coal dust. The succession of clean engines at the head of express trains was widely noted although the speculated reasons for this were not always the same – 'the cleaners have fewer engines to attend to and give more attention to those in commission'. Whatever the reason, and the former seems to be the more plausible, the result was a bonus to rail enthusiast and traveller alike.

There were other improvements, some of which might have resulted from the strange lull of the 'phoney' war which produced an environment that stimulated change. Reading lamps were fitted to improve the lot of passengers travelling after dark. They were simply metal boxes of approved dimensions (12 in long x 6 in wide x 10 in deep) fitted over the centre roof light in each compartment. Two slots were provided in the base of the device to direct a beam of light sufficient for reading onto each of the seats. The blue lamps were still provided and it was acceptable to travel with the reading light switched off and the blind up to allow one to look out on the night scene. On moonlit nights it was a pleasant and seemingly harmless activity, although not all agreed. A comment in *Railways* in March 1940 stated:

> It is surprising to observe what little regard passengers have either for their own safety or that of their fellows. Instances of this can be seen by the number of trains fitted with the improved lighting, going along in the blackout with many of the compartment blinds not drawn down despite the printed requests exhibited in the compartments and elsewhere.

No doubt the defaulters had kept the reading lights on!

It was considered that the initial risks concerning aerial attack had been over-estimated, at least for the time being, and a massive influx of passenger traffic required a better service. Many long distance trains were duplicated daily, the lengths of the trains were increased, and other expresses were added to the timetables. The Southern Railway had reverted to the equivalent of its previous summer timetable with few cancellations within the first two weeks of the wartime restrictions, and by maintaining normal speeds, for four weeks operated the fastest trains in the country.

Even the 'meal hour' stops of important express trains around mid-day were phased out as both the LMS and LNE provided limited restaurant and buffet car facilities (the SR had reintroduced them by the third week of the war!) and they standardized a simple breakfast, luncheon and dinner at half a crown (12 ¹/₂p) for both first and third class passengers. The LMS also introduced a standard service charge in lieu of gratuities and the *Railway Magazine* commented that 'it may be hoped that this will become a regular feature of restaurant car arrangements in future, and the same principle might with advantage be extended by the railway to their hotels (as is the custom abroad).'

The procession of immaculate locomotives heading both goods and passenger trains was very inspiring. Possessing a camera with a focal plane shutter that would capture such trains in action, but prevented from doing so by the War Office restrictions on railway photography, was frustrating. My earlier obsession resurfaced and I had the overwhelming urge to take my chance, at first by quiet country lineside locations near Godley on the old Great Central line, but shortly afterwards at Manchester London Road station where I had previously taken the box camera photographs using the time exposure technique.

The barrier-free LMS arrival platform gave access to my earlier vantage points at the open end of the station. From the relatively concealed position on the lattice girder footbridge I surreptitiously photographed 'Patriot' 5502 as it arrived with an express from Birmingham. On the adjacent platform below, a group of spotters carried their gas masks in box cases slung to the rear – confirmation that the war was really on! It did not take long for me to join them and to realize that no one seemed concerned about a schoolboy taking photographs of trains. I recorded 'Scots' as they came chimney first from Longsight shed and manoeuvred onto the turntable to be aligned for the journey out. The departure provided another splendid photographic opportunity before I crossed over to the LNER where the contrasting forms of Gresley 'Pacifics' and 'Sandringhams' or the older Great Central engines of Robinson's design were equally resplendent in their well-groomed Gorton finish and made other fitting subjects for the camera.

In the many visits to London Road station up to May 1940, I was only challenged on the last occasion when an official on the far side of the tracks bellowed at me as I was about to photograph an incoming 'Scot'. All eyes were on me as the train rumbled past and into the terminus. By the time the last coach had passed my vantage point I had run the length of the adjacent platform and was clear of the station. It did not seem appropriate to risk interrogation!

The LMS Longsight shed was another 'honeypot' and I searched the back streets nearby until I found a gate and access point alongside the main tracks entering the shed by the south end. I asked an amiable railwayman if I could look around and he escorted me to the far side of the shed and then left me with a friendly word of caution to make sure that I took care. 'Patriots', 'Scots', 'Crabs' and other classes of locomotives stood in long rows on the various tracks within the shed, part of which was roofed over and part spanned by massive girders without a roof above. I took pictures and returned home triumphant, delighted to find that the slow shutter had coped well with the lighting conditions within the enclosed shed and I persuaded my brother, Eric, much against his will, to accompany me the following week on another foray. 'We shall be welcomed', I assured him. He was dubious. His unease at Longsight as we stepped through the gate was apparent and scarcely had we set foot across the tracks at the entrance to the shed when an aggressive figure lurched from the shadowy interior, yelling abuse and gesticulating wildly. As this official in black railway uniform made his way towards us, we made a rather rapid and undignified withdrawal. The tirade that followed over the wall indicated that if he had got his hands on us we should have been taken straight to the police – at least that was the gist of his profane remonstrations but his furious ranting was in language couched in a much more basic style!

Manchester and Longsight thus became 'off-limits' and aspirations turned to the old Great Central route across the Pennines to Woodhead. Having travelled regularly along this route on our pre-war excursions to Doncaster we were aware of the many remote localities with splendid lineside vistas that were just asking to be photographed. One of the prime objectives was the picturesque viaduct at Dinting, near Glossop. It spanned Dinting Vale and the station foot-bridge offered a magnificent panoramic view that was vital to any serious photographic record of the line. A half-hour bus ride took me to Dinting where after a steep climb up the path to the station, I was able to take up a suitable stance on the foot-bridge. The bridge was unguarded and I patrolled the foot-bridge casually while keeping an observant eye on the movements of the station staff. As an Up London express approached, I quickly noted that the staff were within the buildings as it was a through train, and the splendid shot of 'Sandringham' No. 2869 *Barnsley* was in the camera.

Shortly afterwards, a stopping suburban train hauled by 2–4–2 tank No. 5579 pulled into the curved platform of the branch line to Glossop. As nobody appeared to be on my side of the track the opportunity was taken to nip along a shallow embankment to a vantage point for the departure. The engine crew both eyed me suspiciously as the photograph was taken and I gave my usual cheery wave and smile to confirm that I wasn't 'the enemy', but as I turned to make my way back to the platform a couple of porters charged round the bend towards me. As they shouted, instinct told me that it wasn't the time or the place for a chat and I bolted up the embankment towards Glossop expecting to run into open country. Instead, I was faced with a few lines of sidings filled with open trucks and close to a small engine shed (the former site, more recently, of the Bahamas Railway Society). There was no locomotive in the yard so I dived under the lines of wagons and tore off down the steep hillside and across the brook to scramble back to the main road to Hyde.

Thinking that the police would by that time have been alerted, it did not seem wise to return to Hyde by the obvious bus route where I might be identified and picked up. Instead, I half ran and half walked up the steep hill, Gamesley Brow, along the road to Marple. At the summit of the climb it felt reasonably safe, but the territory was new to me and it was a considerable surprise to find that the road crossed a high level bridge overlooking the main line and the adjacent Mottram sidings. Wagons trickled downhill from a gentle push over the hump and threaded their way through the vast array of sorting tracks under the control of a signal-box alongside the first junction and almost below the bridge. After a furtive glance around, another valued shot was in the camera and the brisk walk to Marple continued as before, away from the possible search parties. The camera was by this time safely stowed beneath my coat for the eight mile trek that circuited round to home. Of course, had there been a search, the Marple Road would just as easily have been scoured as the road to Hyde, but I was a jump ahead. They wouldn't search the Marple Road for someone who lived in Hyde. With that naïve thought in mind, I made my escape.

The rapidly deteriorating war situation had caused the sudden change of mood demonstrated by my pursuers. Norway, Denmark, Holland, Belgium and France had all fallen before the onslought of the Blitzkrieg and after Dunkirk there was much talk of spies and a 'Fifth Column'. Railway photography became more severely restricted. The railways were military objectives – none disputed that. From that time, station photography was out of the question as the whole country was put onto the alert. Churchill replaced Chamberlain and the nation responded to his call. The imminent and very real concern was the threat of an invasion and every line of defence had to be explored. Not least was the proposal to confuse any of the enemy who landed by removing all place-names. All signs or notices that indicated localities had to be eliminated.

The railways responded by the removal of destination boards and other place-name indicators from all the stations. This involved the removal of not only the standard name boards, but name-plates from platform seats, station building windows, lamp-posts and signal-boxes, and even those names outlined in flowers, box hedges or stone at some country stations. On the LNER alone a total of 21,000 name signs was reported as being obliterated. From then on, the public relied on clear vocal calls from the porters by day as well as by night if they were not familiar with the halt.

For the remainder of that glorious summer of 1940 I took to remote spots in the Pennines where I could lurk behind some wall or bush as the train approached, step out to take the picture, and give a friendly wave to any observant driver to reassure him. My excursions grew longer as I followed remote paths up into the hills on the approach to Woodhead where my clandestine lineside activities could take place in vast open tracts of country into which I could disappear at will. There were superb viewpoints where shots could be planned in advance without outside interference.

Work on the overhead electrification of the line had commenced in 1938 but had been halted by the war. In the upper parts of Longdendale the support stanchions and cross girders had already been erected and remained thus until the post-war years. They were protected by red lead which had weathered to a shade of pink but after reported fears that these would aid the navigation of enemy aircraft, a gang of men was hurriedly put to work to paint them black, another of the 'Armchair Brigade' decisions which any air-crew of the time in all likelihood would have derided. With such magnificent aids to navigation as the string of reservoirs down the length of Longdendale and the gleaming rails of the track alongside, any lineside posts, pink or black, would never have been apparent from the heights at which the aircraft would have flown across the Pennines. My own observations at the time recall them being painted grey which was a sensible neutral colour. Of course I was thinking about their intrusion onto my photographs of the line. As far as possible, they were to be avoided!

The 'Woodhead Line', as it was locally dubbed, provided a perfect setting for my wartime railway photography. The landscape was so vast that there was no need to hide or look over one's shoulder before taking a shot – an approaching figure could be observed at a good distance and any compromising situation was thereby avoided. Added to that, the line was extremely busy, the line occupation being as dense as any in the country except perhaps for those commuter lines around London. This considerable flow of traffic had led to the installation of lengthy stretches of loop accommodation where the very slow and heavy coal trains could await the opportunity to leapfrog a short distance along the main line to the next loop. Great care was required in bringing the heavy coal trains down from Woodhead because of the ever present danger of a train going out of control on the steep gradients should the engine brakes fail. It was custom-ary for a number of wagon brakes to be pinned down at Dunford Bridge before the west-ern descent. The guard's van brakes were also kept on as the coal train crept downhill at a very slow pace while the chosen brake wagons screeched loudly in protest as the train passed. One fireman was severely rebuked by the driver for opening the regulator to move off from one of the loop halts when the line was signalled clear. The sheer weight of the train was sufficient to push it forwards on the downhill stretch when the engine brakes were released. As an added precaution, the loop adjacent to Valehouse signal-box led to a sand drag which extended almost to Hadfield East.

While the severe gradients restricted the speed of the climb to Woodhead and severe curves restricted speeds on the descent, the real bottleneck of the route was at Woodhead where the first single bore tunnel was opened in 1845 and the second bore in 1852. Extensive waiting loops at the western approach eased the congestion of the main line and were invariably occupied by one or more goods trains waiting for the opportunity to slip through. The tunnels were just over three miles in length and involved a gradient of 1 in 201. The Up tunnel was notorious for the dense, choking, sulphurous fumes from successive engines as they pounded up the climb. Those held within the loops below the entrance had to start from scratch and it was the up tunnel that bore the brunt of this continuous blasting of its surface walls throughout the twenty-four hours of almost every day throughout the year. Engines struggled to the summit which lay just before the exit on the eastern side. Visibility was invariably almost zero and a clanking bell indicated to the driver that the engine had passed that point. Passengers could also hear this brief signal as the mechanical contraption was probably activated by a lever catching the passing train. Incredibly, in 1902, an attempt was made to operate a signal-box within the up tunnel but even a reduced shift would not tempt many men to staff the cabin. It was almost impossible to see the tail lamp of any train that passed or for any driver to observe a signal. Yet the cabin was operated until 1909 when it was no longer possible to staff it, no doubt because of the quality of the air!

Despite the provision of ventilation shafts, one of which dominated the hillside just above the western entrance, the choking fumes persisted throughout the Up tunnel for the full century that it was in use. Any heavy train brought to a halt on the Up climb invariably had great difficulty in starting again and it is on record that during the Second World War one driver of a stalled passenger train became confused, mistook his direction, and propelled the train backwards out of the tunnel.

This continuous blasting of the walls of the Up tunnel with the acid-laden fumes caused not only the crumbling of the mortar of the tunnel lining but considerable erosion of the rails as well. To enable the necessary repairs to be undertaken, it became customary for the Up tunnel to be closed on Sundays. Single line working in either direction was operated through the Down tunnel on such days as the repair unit train blocked the Up line.

The long treks necessary to record the railway in Longendale terminated at Crowden. Not until the late autumn of 1940, when I purchased a second-hand bicycle, was I able to cover more ground. Although Woodhead then became within practical reach, photographs of the tunnel entrance could not be contemplated. It was defended as any major military objective was in those troubled days. Armed soldiers stood on guard at the entrance and the whole area must have been considered a prohibited zone as far as photography was concerned. My aspirations had to be satisfied by a shot of *Solario* as the 'Pacific' made its approach alongside the reserve loops some way below the tunnel mouth.

A brief sortie over the moors to Dunford Bridge revealed that the eastern end of the tunnel was equally well patrolled and I toiled back up the steep moorland road without a pictorial record of the eastern portals of the tunnel. A stark wind-pruned hawthorn made a splendid silhouette against the evening sky and with a yellow colour filter to enhance the clouds, a very dramatic picture was produced.

I had earlier photographed a friend's models of German aircraft suspended by thin threads against a white cloudy sky. It was easy to superimpose one of these models onto the tree picture and a realistic image was created. A further print was made, this time with the enemy aircraft plunging out of control, a plume of smoke following in its wake. The smoke was 'borrowed' from a train 'somewhere in Longendale'.

I was a working man by this time having commenced in September as a junior cost clerk at Adamson's engineering works, Hyde, for the princely sum of 13s. 10d. (69p) per week. The photograph depicting the last moments of a Heinkel 111 'shot down over the moors' much impressed one of the directors, Mr Flynn, who purchased the print for a pound. No doubt he enjoyed spinning a line or two about the photograph when he made his periodic business trips to America. For my part, with the bicycle, the camera, and a pound in my pocket, I was fast becoming 'upwardly mobile'.

0–4–4T of the former Midland Railway No. 1416 at London Road station. Engines of this type normally worked the push-and-pull service to Wilmslow.

Well-groomed LMS 'Royal Scot' class 7P 4–6–0 No. 6163 *Civil Service Rifleman* stands by at Manchester London Road station. For a period the schoolboy photographer was able to take such photographs quite openly as nobody challenged what was, in those days, a relatively rare pursuit.

Even after seven months of war the locomotives on passenger services were still well maintained and kept immaculate – a condition due, in part, to the reduction in services that was imposed initially, leaving a surplus of labour at the maintenance depots. Increasing demands for locomotives soon reversed this position as the war progressed and traffic flowed at a far higher rate than before the war. LMS 'Royal Scot' class 7P 4–6–0 No. 6126 *Royal Army Service Corps* has just arrived from Longsight shed and faces the wrong way for the outward journey.

LMS 'Royal Scot' class 7P 4–6–0 No. 6126 rotating on the LMS turntable at Manchester London Road station.

The motion of LMS 'Royal Scot' No. 6126 *Royal Army Service Corps* is well displayed as the loco-motive quietly backs down onto its train.

Departure time at Manchester London Road and *Royal Army Service Corps* makes an impressive start on a suburban stopping train to Crewe.

Prior to the war the locomotive bringing in the crack Marylebone–Manchester express would remain at the buffer stops until the station pilot tank engine drew out the coaches. The express locomotive would then travel light engine to Gorton Tank. By March 1940, the sixth month of the war, the LNE appeared to be following the neighbouring LMS practice in that A1 'Pacific' No. 2554 *Woolwinder* backed out while still attached to the train as the pilot tank took the lead. The rear lamp on the engine, the signal and the 'look out' positions of both engine and train crew indicate the movement.

The increasing length of wartime trains brought occasional double heading of express trains from departure platform A at Manchester London Road. LNER class B2 No. 5426 *City of Chester* in apple green livery prepares to leave with black liveried B7 No. 5033 in the lead. Both locomotives were designed by John G. Robinson of the former Great Central Railway.

LNER class B2 No. 5426 *City of Chester*, still relatively immaculate after six months of war, had obviously been involved in some minor mishap indicated by the downward bent forward edge of the running plate. The magnificent appearance of these locomotives was not matched by their performance and they were generally assigned to secondary expresses that made less demand on haulage capacity and speed. They often headed cross-country expresses such as the Manchester–Cleethorpes or Lincoln services. Double heading was almost invariable on the heavier trains. There is little doubt that the war extended the life-span of this class of locomotive.

The LNER class B7 was Robinson's final and much appreciated 4–6–0 design and No. 5033 was allocated to Sheffield from 1929 to 1943. It was regularly seen on the Manchester to Sheffield route via Woodhead. The locomotive was a 5 ft 8 in version of the 'Lord Faringdon' B3 four-cylinder express locomotive designed for the Great Central Railway and whereas only six of the latter were built, thirty-eight of the mixed traffic engines were constructed, the final ten after grouping.

Old and new at Manchester London Road station as LNER class D10 No. 5438 *Worsley–Taylor*, one of Robinson's original 'Director' 4–4–0s, arrives with a train from Cleethorpes as Gresley's B17 4–6–0 No. 2869 *Barnsley* prepares to depart with the early afternoon express for London Marylebone.

At Gorton the B17s were very unpopular, probably because of the rough riding on the severe gradients and curves of the Woodhead route, but they were nevertheless subjected to the most rigorous cleaning at the shed. Seven months after the start of the war No. 2869 *Barnsley* glistened with the pristine finish that had been applied in preparation for its run on the London Marylebone express. Although the tender of the 'Footballer' was larger than the earlier B17s, the policy of stacking the coal to a height above the level of the cab followed old practice from the days when the smaller tenders had insufficient capacity for the route.

The distant gantry signals the line clear for LNER class F1 2–4–2T No. 5577 as it struggles out of the Manchester London Road station with a suburban passenger train for Hayfield. No. 5577 was one of the original F1 locomotives designed and built by Parker in 1889 for the Manchester Sheffield and Lincolnshire Railway. It was subsequently modified by Robinson for the Great Central Railway. In the foreground Stanier 'Black Five' 4–6–0 No. 5245 glides into the LMS arrival platform with an express from the Midlands.

An un-named 'Patriot' class 6P5F No. 5542 prepares to depart as 'Royal Scot' class 7P 4–6–0 No. 6163 *Civil Service Rifleman* arrives with an express from Birmingham. Up to this point a youthful appearance had allowed the schoolboy author to get away with his early wartime photography at Manchester London Road station, but the irate company official who can be seen bellowing a warning across the tracks, prompted a decision to end such open activities. A rapid withdrawal was inevitable and by the time the arriving train had passed the vantage point, the author had disappeared into the crowded streets of Manchester. No further pictures were taken at Manchester London Road after that incident and it was accepted as a prohibited area in view of the seriously deteriorating war situation in May 1940.

The staff were quite welcoming on this first visit to Longsight shed where rows of locomotives were lined up in various stages of preparation for the next run. There was no restriction on movement or photography and even the roofed-over section had sufficient light to allow pictures to be taken. In contrast, London's Euston station had such an effective permanent blackout that artificial lighting was required throughout the day. In this photograph of the covered section of the shed, Johnson's Midland 0–6–0 class 3F design, No. 3400, stands to the fore. The Belpaire firebox was part of Fowler's modification during rebuilding of the 1885 design. To the left, class 5 2–6–0 No. 2815 is positioned ahead of a sister engine and an unidentified 'Patriot' occupies the centre road.

Shed visits provided one of the few occasions when it was possible to take a front view of a loco-motive from the track. 'Patriot' class 6P5F No. 5545 *Planet* is viewed from a position at the head of an inspection pit within the covered section of Longsight shed.

The one successful visit to Longsight shed has produced what is probably the only wartime record of that place and this photograph shows one of several rows of locomotives in the open-roofed section. Un-named 'Patriot' class 6P5F No. 5542 stands at the head of a line of well-groomed engines. Rails lifted from the adjacent track lie alongside.

'Patriot' class 6P5F 4–6–0 No. 5502 *Royal Naval Division* stands at the head of a line of locomotives that reflect the high standard of maintenance still applied at Longsight shed at the end of May 1940.

Close shot of the motion of 'Patriot' class 6P5F 4–6–0 No. 5502 *Royal Naval Division* which was one of many of the class within Longsight shed on the occasion of this one visit at the end of May 1940. By the following week, in the aftermath of Dunkirk, the mood had changed and strangers who lurked with cameras were viewed with more than suspicion. The next attempt to gain entrance and repeat the experience met with a very aggressive reception and no further shed visits were undertaken.

London and North Western Railway class 7F 0–8–0 No. 9224 quietly simmers at the head of a line of sister engines within the open section of Longsight shed. The tarpaulin blackout screen can be seen neatly folded back on the roof of the cab. On the adjacent track, the cab of LMS class 4F 0–6–0 No. 4303 is just visible.

Close shot of the motion of Stanier 'Black Five' class No. 5350 taken on a brief visit to Manchester Central station. The receding angle avoided the main station buildings classified as an important military objective and it also helped the photographer to conceal his activities in such a public place.

A remote bridge which spanned the newly ballasted tracks of the lines to Stockport Tiviot Dale (left) and to Bredbury and Manchester (right) provided an undisturbed vantage point for this picture of an empty coal train hauled by Midland 0–6–0 locomotive No. 3969. The immaculate condition of the tracks and signals and the well-maintained class 4F locomotive on this approach to Romiley may seem surprising considering that the picture was taken when Britain stood alone and the Battle of Britain was being fought in the skies. Within six months a Messerschmitt 109 would be displayed in the grounds of council offices near the distant houses as part of the fund-raising effort in support of the RAF.

Another photograph taken from the bridge near Romiley as an unidentified LMS 'Crab' 2–6–0 approaches Romiley junction on the Tiviot Dale line. A third line to the junction is visible at the top right of the photograph. This was the old Great Central line from Manchester to Macclesfield. It was spanned by the same bridge from which the photograph was taken and all three lines merged at the junction before Romiley station.

The merging of the three lines is apparent in this eastward looking view from the bridge. Stanier 'Black Five' 4–6–0 No. 5238 hauls a goods train along the Bredbury Manchester line after passing the triple junction which lies beyond the signals near Romiley station.

An unidentified LNER C13 4–4–2T hauling a suburban train to Macclesfield is silhouetted against the snow as it crosses Marple Viaduct over the River Goyt. The viaduct's twelve stone arches were constructed in 1863 and stand 124 ft above the river. The Peak Forest Canal Aqueduct, completed in 1808, stands to the fore.

THE WOODHEAD LINE, 1940 TO 1942
LNER

The 'Woodhead line' as it was frequently called took its name from what was, through-out LNER days, the fourth longest tunnel in the country at 3 miles 24 yd. The western approach to the tunnel was through some of the most attractive scenery in the north of England and the line climbed to an altitude of 1,000 ft near the eastern exit of the Woodhead Tunnel at Dunford Bridge. Severe weather conditions often prevailed in these wild moorland areas and during the war a group of soldiers trekked from the railway across the frozen expanse of the Woodhead Reservoir to the George and Dragon on the far shore, thinking that they were walking across fields. The former landlord, Eddie Bagshaw, frequently recalled this incident in the days before the hostelry was demolished.

From its origins as the Sheffield, Ashton-under-Lyne and Manchester Railway, and by amalgamation, the Manchester Sheffield and Lincolnshire Railway, the line became part of the Great Central Railway in 1897 and was taken over by the LNER in 1923. From these mixed origins the line drew its motive power and provided the rich diversity of locomotives from the graceful lines of the 'Jersey Lily Atlantic' and other Robinson designs to Gresley's superb 'Pacifics'. The proposed electrification of the line was brought to a halt in 1940 when the war stopped all connected work and it is during the subsequent years when wartime emergencies made unprecedented demands that the line was recorded as depicted in this work. The photographs in this section are in sequence of location from Newton to Woodhead.

The fence adjacent to the goal-posts on the 'lower pitch' sports field at Hyde Grammar School was a favoured spot during schooltime games and provided this view of LNER A1 'Pacific' No. 4474 *Victor Wild* as it approached Newton station with the crack Manchester London Road–London Marylebone express

The Glossop push-and-pull propelled by class C13 4–4–2T No. 5193 on the Up journey from Manchester London Road passes the open fence boundary of the Hyde Grammar School sports field where the author took more interest in the passing trains than in the game of football. Angry pursuits by more enthusiastic fellow pupils frequently led to escape within Hyde Park where the arch 'folly' led to an equally satisfactory vantage point from which to observe the railway. This photograph from the bridge that spanned the tracks by Newton signal-box shows the loading gauge over the short siding alongside the school fence and the white-washed buffer stop painted thus in accordance with blackout regulations. The driver's window and outer bell can be seen at the front end of the leading twelve-wheeled bogie coach of the push-and-pull. This open third class vehicle with the central door was a great favourite with regular travellers. It gave a remarkably smooth ride and the large windows offered much enhanced views. The shunter to the right of the picture carries his uncoupling pole to assist with the shunting operations in progress at Newton as the auto-train passes.

A friendly signalman, Mr Eccles, allowed the schoolboy author to operate the signals controlling the line between Godley Arches and the approach to Hyde junction under his close supervision. A highly enlightened games master at Hyde Grammar School approved these visits to the signal-box during the games sessions in the final year at school. This shot depicts the light frame levers while two lineside workmen enjoy a short break. Pneumatic signalling had been installed from Manchester to Newton in the Great Central days of 1923. Signal-boxes to the east of Newton operated with the heavy levers that were more typical. The high polish and immaculate state of the signal-box were matched by Mr Eccles's elegant copper-plate writing in the official log.

LNER A1 'Pacific' No. 2558 *Tracery* viewed from the signal-box at Newton as it passes with the down London Marylebone–Manchester express early in 1942. Its high-sided LNER tender has been replaced by an old Great Northern type with the coal rails along the top edge.

LNER class A4 'Pacifics' were relatively unknown on the Woodhead line apart from Sir Nigel Gresley's brief visit with an exhibition train *en route* to Manchester in 1938. An unusual wartime visitor, No. 4495 *Golden Fleece* was spotted as it manoeuvred as a light engine on the track alongside Newton signal-box, much of which is concealed by the steam. The engine faced Manchester on the Down line but its movements thereafter were not recorded. This photograph was taken later than the others in this series covering the Woodhead line during the war but the Garter blue on the locomotive and the absence of the side skirting indicates that it was taken early in December 1941. Later that month it received the wartime livery of overall black without linings. The signal-box and goods shed on the adjacent platform are now demolished.

LNER class C13 4–4–2T No. 5310 leaves Newton station with an Up Manchester to Glossop and Hadfield passenger train. The line immediately crossed Newton Arches over 'Sammy's Pit', a favoured local fishing pond which was filled in after the war. The bogie stock replaced the former six-wheeled carriages that were characteristic of the former Great Central suburban services.

LNER class K3 2–6–0 No. 3816 storms up the bank approaching Godley Arches with an unmarked express. This photograph was taken early in 1940 from a quiet lineside location which we called 'The Box' because of a ballast container which provided both seat and viewpoint in the short breaks between trains. It was thought prudent at the time to operate the camera in such relatively secluded spots. An open wooden fence to the rear allowed for a rapid exodus across the fields.

As part of the up-grading of engines on the former Great Central route into Manchester, LNER 2–6–2 class V2s were introduced alongside the 'Pacifics' shortly before the war. No. 4841 of this class makes easy work with a heavy London express as it climbs alongside 'The Box' near Godley.

Working hard with a moderate load LNER class J11 0–6–0 No. 5236 storms up the bank towards Godley Arches. These engines were nicknamed 'Pom-Poms' as they first came into service at a time when the pom-pom gun was being used by the Boers during the South African War.

LNER class B17 4–6–0 No. 2849 *Sheffield United* coasts downhill past 'The Box' with the Down Marylebone–Manchester express on the final seven-mile stretch to London Road station. With the introduction of the A1 'Pacifics' onto this crack express in 1939, the 'Sandringhams' were less involved. The tall chimney of Walls' Ice-cream factory (now demolished) marks the point where the line crosses the Hyde–Mottram road at Godley Arches.

The 'Immingham' 4–6–0s appeared in 1906, designed for express passenger working with their 6 ft 7 in driving wheels. Only ten were built and here LNER B4 No. 6102, resplendent in apple green, approaches Godley with an Up train of coal empties destined for the Yorkshire or Nottinghamshire pits.

Robinson's first 4–6–0 design was the class 8 of which fourteen were built and all survived the war years. With 6 ft 1 in coupled wheels they were designed for working fast goods, particularly the fish trains from Grimsby to Manchester and elsewhere which earned them their nickname of 'fish engines'. Known by the LNER as class B5, No. 5183 approaches Newton with a Down freight in the early summer of 1940.

As the buds open in early April 1940 LNER A1 'Pacific' No. 4478 *Hermit* passes 'The Box' with the 2.20 p.m. Up Marylebone express. *Hermit* was the third A1 'Pacific' to be allocated to Gorton shed and partnered *Tracery* and *Victor Wild* from March 1939. *Solario* and *Woolwinder* also moved to Gorton later that same year.

No. 4474 *Victor Wild* was the second LNER A1 'Pacific' to be allocated to Gorton (February 1939) and it partnered the other A1s on the crack Marylebone expresses. It was the Gorton policy always to have a named engine on these turns. In the midsummer of 1940 *Victor Wild* pounds up the bank towards Godley with the 2.20 p.m. Up Marylebone express, the exhaust almost invisible in the summer heat.

LNER A1 'Pacific' No. 4473 *Solario* looking moderately clean but without the high polish of the earlier years, an indication of the harder times that lie ahead. In the high summer of 1940 the Down Marylebone–Manchester express coasts past 'The Box' on the final stretch to London Road station.

LNER class C13 4–4–2T replaced the F1 2–4–2T which had hauled the six-wheeled suburban coaches from the turn of the century. The introduction of old bogie stock onto the suburban services shortly before the war required more powerful engines and over twenty of this class were allocated to Gorton Tank. They took over virtually all the London Road suburban trains. No. 5193 was one of several equipped with the push-and-pull vacuum gear for working the auto-trains to Glossop and Hadfield and is shown passing 'The Box' on its Down return to Manchester London Road with the twin car push-and-pull unit.

A woodland area provided cover close to the line above Godley junction and A1 'Pacific' No. 4474 *Victor Wild* on the Down Marylebone–Manchester express was among the first wartime photographs taken with the 'Purma Special' early in 1940. What could or could not be photographed was a matter of conjecture and discretion favoured the brief sortie from a concealed lineside position.

A4 No. 4488 *Union of South Africa* put in an appearance on the Up London express in February 1942 and the attempt to record it passing 'The Box' was frustrated by the passing of a goods train on the near Down track. By running towards Godley Arches a receding view of the locomotive captured the historic scene as the train pounds up the bank towards the smoking chimney of Walls' Ice-cream factory alongside the viaduct. The visit was regarded as a 'one-off' event and not until after the war was it learned that *Union of South Africa* had spent a month on the line and might have been photographed under less wintry conditions! Within two months the Garter blue livery would be replaced by the overall black without lining as prescribed by the exigencies of wartime. The stainless steel band along the lower rim of the aerofoil and tender was matched along each coach on the pre-war 'Coronation' express. The richly painted panel bearing the coat of arms of South Africa is prominent on the cabside beneath the stainless steel figures of the engine number.

LNER class B17 4–6–0 No. 2869 *Barnsley* heads an unidentified Up express on the climb through Godley. The station-master's house was the detached building below the embankment and was positioned on Station Road about a quarter of a mile below the station. A row of cottages was provided for the other staff who worked at the station or in the sidings at Godley junction.

LNER class K3 2–6–0 No. 2458 and an unidentified sister engine double head a train of coal empties on the up track alongside Walls' Ice-cream factory and Godley sidings. Loaded coal trains on the Down track tended to be shorter as it made them easier to control and the locomotives frequently paired on the return trip with the empties.

LNER class K3 2–6–0 No. 3815 heads a Down slow goods train on its cautious descent through the Hattersley cutting on the approach to Godley junction.

LNER class V2 2–6–2 No. 4888 takes a turn on the Up Marylebone express and storms up the bank beyond Hattersley cutting on the approach to Broadbottom.

Class A1 No. 4478 *Hermit* at speed on the 3.20 p.m. Down Marylebone–Manchester express as it sweeps round the curve towards Hattersley cutting. The iron bridge in the background was a favourite unobtrusive site during the early stages of the author's wartime railway photography in 1940.

An eastward looking receding shot from the bridge as No. 2562 *Isinglass* heads through Broadbottom. The neat black and white lining applied to the LNER apple green of the tender is clearly seen.

LNER 2–4–2T class F1 No. 5582 approaches the iron bridge at Broadbottom with a suburban train for Glossop and Hadfield. Built at Gorton in 1891, this locomotive worked through the war and was not withdrawn until 1949.

A newcomer to the line, class A1 'Pacific' No. 2562 *Isinglass* approaches the iron bridge with an unidentified express in June 1940. The heaped coal in the tender and the immaculate condition of the locomotive confirm that Gorton Tank maintained their pre-war standards.

North Eastern locomotives double head an Up train of coal empties with an unidentified class Q7, said to be Britain's most handsome 0–8–0, piloting a Q6 0–8–0, one of Vincent Raven's long-lived heavy goods locomotives. The tarpaulin sheeting required at night to screen the glare from the firebox is neatly tied back at the top rim of each cab.

4–4–2 class 4 Robinson-designed 'Atlantic' No. 6083 in shining black livery, blows off steam as it coasts through Broadbottom with an unidentified wartime express in July 1940. This much-admired Robinson design had such graceful lines that it acquired the nickname 'Jersey Lily'.

Class B17 4–6–0 No. 2866 *Nottingham Forest* sweeps through Broadbottom with another unidentified wartime Down express on a July afternoon in 1940. The name-plates of the 'Footballers' were
unique as the centre splashers carried a cast half section of a football, embellished on either side
with panels displaying the club colours, an excellent example of the flair for publicity characteristic
of the pre-war LNER.

LNER 2–6–2 class V2 No. 4834 on the Up London Marylebone express passes a Down goods as it emerges from beneath the iron bridge at Broadbottom. Tarpaulin covers were frequently tied down over the open trucks.

LNER 2–6–0 class K3 No. 1162 hauls a lengthy slow goods on the Up line through Broadbottom. The use of tarpaulin covers on the open trucks may have been for the purpose of concealment as much as for protection.

Ivatt's Great Northern 4–4–2 'Atlantic' No. 4425, class C4 of the LNER, invariably worked the Liverpool–Hull expresses. The Up train here passes under the bridge at Broadbottom.

On an early summer's afternoon in June 1940 A1 'Pacific' No. 4478 *Hermit* pounds gracefully up the bank towards Broadbottom as it hauls the 2.20 p.m. Up Marylebone express.

One of the most impressive heavy goods engines to traverse the Pennines, Robinson's Great Central 2–8–0 design, was a classic. It proved its robust and capable nature by being chosen as one of the standard War Department engines in the First World War and was still well up to requirements for active service in the Second World War. LNER class O4 No. 6186 carefully makes its way through Broadbottom with a Down mixed goods.

2–6–0 No. 4004, one of the original ten Great Northern K3 locomotives, starts up after a brief halt at the signal and cautiously opens up to round the bend below the iron bridge with a Down mixed goods. From the footplate, a gold-braided inspector views the photographer with an air of uncertainty in this brief encounter in March 1940. By midsummer the signal arms would be converted to upper quadrant.

LNER 4–6–0 class B3 No. 6165 *Valour* was the Great Central Memorial engine. It invariably ran from Manchester to Sheffield on Remembrance Day (11 November) bearing wreaths of poppies on the name-plates and the smokebox door. The pristine condition of those early days has been eclipsed by the grime of the present war but the large shield-shaped name-plate can just be seen. In addition to the very elaborate lettering of its name, the plate also bore the following legend in small letters:' In memory of Great Central Railway employees who gave their lives for their country 1914–1918.' The unscheduled express was probably a troop train.

The early stages of wartime neglect and restricted maintenance fail to suppress the splendid lines of this unidentified LNER B7 on a slow mixed goods as it makes its way on the Down line through Broadbottom.

An unidentified Robinson 2–8–0 LNER class O4 crosses Mottram Viaduct with an Up slow goods. The lengthy spans of the viaduct between the original stone piers were shortened by additional brick piers to take the increased weight of the trains. The viaduct's correct name is Besthill Viaduct, although locals generally refer to it as 'Broadbottom Arches'. Other viaducts on the route – Newton, Godley and Dinting – are also called 'arches', although only Newton and Godley retain that structure throughout.

Mottram yard was planned during the final years of Lord Faringdon's life, when he was the deputy chairman of the LNER, and was opened in 1935. It was capable of carrying out all the marshalling previously undertaken at Guide Bridge and Godley, and in far less time. Congestion in the Woodhead loops was greatly reduced by this development and the trains were able to move more freely. The author came across this viewpoint by accident when making an escape from pursuit after a photographic session at Dinting.

An unidentified LNER 0–6–0 class J39 trundles a Down mixed goods over the high span of Broadbottom Arches some 120 ft above the River Etherow at the deep gorge excavated as a glacial overflow channel. The alternate kerbstones painted white and the similar bands painted on the road bridge and at the bottom of the viaduct pier were to assist the limited road traffic under conditions of blackout. In those conditions vehicles were required to mask their headlamps with covers that restricted the light beam to three slits diverted to the ground.

LNER 4–6–0 class B17 No. 2869 *Barnsley* crosses Dinting Viaduct with an Up Manchester–
Cleethorpes express. The splendid and scenic viaduct spans Dinting Vale at heights reaching 121 ft
and care was required to avoid being seen when taking the photograph as it was classified as a
military objective and, therefore, taboo. Black paint obscures the top section of the station gas lamp
to meet the blackout requirement that light beams may only be directed downwards. The station
nameboard was still prominent in April 1940 but by June any reference to place-names had been
obliterated.

Veteran Great Central 2–4–2T of 1889, now LNER class F1 No. 5579 with an extended service life due to the war, sets out round the severe curve of the Glossop branch as it leaves Dinting station. From Glossop it will reverse bunker first to take the right hand junction of the Dinting triangle to Hadfield from which point it will return chimney first down the main line for a second stop at Dinting and thence across the viaduct and on to Manchester. Just after this picture was taken the photographer was pursued by the station staff who must have been alerted. As they came round the embankment a rapid exodus was required and a lengthy escape route was followed to avoid capture!

LNER class A1 'Pacific' No. 2562 *Isinglass* on an unidentified Up express after passing Dinting station. The topping of coal on the tender indicates that Gorton still retained its standard practice. The coaches are a mixed stock with one of the Great Central 'Barnum' coaches with elaborate brass handrails in the lead. Gresley teak coaches and three green and cream tourist coaches make up the rest of the train.

LNER class A1 'Pacific' No. 4474 *Victor Wild* with a Down London Marylebone–Manchester express passing Hadfield. The twin articulated coaches at the head of the train are the pre-war LNER green and cream tourist coaches.

The large boiler and wide firebox of Ivatt's 'Atlantic' are very apparent on this class C1 4–4–2, No. 4425, passing through Hadfield on its regular working of the Liverpool–Hull express. The distant latticed stanchions and cross spars had been erected in 1939 as part of the electrification scheme of the Manchester–Sheffield line and strengthened to enable them to span the considerable number of tracks from the main line to the adjacent sidings. The work was halted at the outbreak of the war and was not resumed until some years afterwards.

An unidentified LNER class J39 0–6–0 blows off steam as it coasts along the main line with a Down mixed goods and is ignored by the free range poultry in the adjacent field on the approach to Hadfield. The remote footpaths through this section of Longdendale gave access to some splendid lineside locations away from wartime human interference.

The splendour of this Gresley 'Pacific' is not lost despite its mundane task of hauling empty coal trucks. Wartime emergency measures require such service and LNER class A1 4–6–2 No. 4477 *Gay Crusader* clearly masters the task despite the visible signs of a need for maintenance. The Down slow loop line in the foreground has a sand drag adjacent to it as a safety precaution against any runaway loaded coal train on the descent. It stretched from Valehouse to a point approaching Hadfield East signal-box.

As A1 'Pacific' No. 2543 *Melton* sweeps round the curve at Valehouse with an unidentified Down express, the sand drag on the Down slow loop is very apparent in the foreground. Valehouse signal-box can just be seen by the signals towards the rear of the train.

Showing scorch marks on the smokebox door but otherwise in a reasonably clean state, class D11 4–4–0 No. 5502 *Zeebrugge* glides round the bend alongside Valehouse signal-box with safety valve blowing off. The Down Cleethorpes–Manchester express takes the fast line where the track divides opposite the signal-box to provide the slow loop for goods traffic. The additional point in the foreground is the emergency safeguard whereby any runaway coal train could be diverted onto the sand drag which extended almost to Hadfield.

Travel-stained LNER class O4 2–8–0 No. 6384 makes the traditional very slow and cautious descent through the short cutting to Valehouse signal-box where it will be diverted to the slow loop to Hadfield. Unfitted heavy goods could push the train forwards from a stand as soon as the engine brakes were released even though some of the wagons had their brakes pinned down. Drivers exercised great care to ensure that the descent was entirely under their control. At this cutting the up line branched to a supporting loop to keep the main line clear of the slow moving goods on the climb. The rusted points in the left foreground activated an emergency diversion to safeguard the up main line against the risk of any runaway wagons. The high level Woodhead to Glossop road can be seen along the flank of Peaknaze Moor close to Devil's Elbow, a notorious bend just off the right of the picture.

Class A1 'Pacific' No. 4478 *Hermit* runs freely on the downhill stretch approaching Valehouse with the Down London Marylebone–Manchester express in tow. The green and cream tourist buffet coach in the centre of the train followed the restoration of limited catering on long distance routes. Peaknaze Moor, at 1,453 ft, towers over 600 ft above the track at this point but by the time the line has climbed through the tunnel at Woodhead, it will have reached 1,000 ft.

LNER 2–6–0 class K3 No. 2439 climbs away from the cutting above Valehouse with an Up stopping train to Sheffield. The varied stock includes a 'Barnum' coach, the elegant brass handrails of which are clearly visible in the centre of the train.

An unidentified LNER B17 4–6–0, one of the 'Footballers', heads an Up express for Cleethorpes above Rhodeswood Reservoir.

A string of light engines piloted by one of Robinson's popular mixed traffic 4–6–0 engines, LNER class B7 No. 5462, with a Great Eastern 0–6–0 No. 8280 and a Great Central 2–8–0 No. 6547 in tow, makes its way on the Up line near Torside. The deep pink of the red lead paint, applied to the stanchions and cross spars of the electrification scheme for their protection, had faded to a pale pink. The 'authorities' decided that they should be painted black after reported fears that they would aid the navigation of enemy aircraft. The author's memory recalls a neutral shade of grey following the pink.

A great appetite for coal initiated nicknames for the former Great Central class 9Q mixed traffic 4–6–0s and they were known as 'Black Pigs' or 'Miners' Friends' in consequence. These names were never used at Gorton Tank where the men had a very great regard for this splendid locomotive. LNER class B7, No. 5482, has that well-maintained Gorton appearance as it drifts towards Valehouse with this Down mixed goods.

An unidentified Robinson LNER class O4 2–8–0 approaching Torside with an Up train of coal empties. The hillside drops immediately below the line to the Rhodeswood Reservoir.

One of Robinson's Great Central 'Tinies', despite its age, masters the grade on the fast Up line on the approach to Torside with a mixed freight in tow. LNER class Q4 No. 5163 makes an impressive picture high above Rhodeswood Reservoir just visible below the front buffer.

LNER class B17 4–6–0 'Footballer' No. 2861 *Sheffield Wednesday*, as immaculate as it was in the days of the 'Continental Boat Express' but this time taking a troop special over part of the same route as it climbs towards Torside.

Another troop train hauled by one of the original Great Central 'Directors', LNER class D10 4–4–0 No. 5438 *Worsley-Taylor*, pounds up the curve approaching Torside. The cut-away cab side is the distinguishing feature that identifies this older class from the new 'Directors'.

LNER class A1 'Pacific' No. 2562 *Isinglass* and the Up Manchester – London Marylebone express still maintain the well-groomed appearance that signified the 'Gorton touch' a year after the declaration of war.

The number on the cab, the only part of the engine that has been cleaned, reveals the identity of this A1 'Pacific' as No. 4473 *Solario*. The blitz of 1940 to 1941 brought the distant war in Europe much nearer to home. Clean and well-maintained engines were a luxury that could no longer be taken for granted. Among the varied rake of coaches on this Up express near Torside, the second vehicle can be identified by the ornate brass handrails as one of the 'Barnum' coaches.

Sweeping round the curve below Torside level crossing, LNER class B17 4–6–0 No. 2869 *Barnsley* lacks the lustre of the previous year but the wartime reduction of maintenance is only just beginning.

LNER class A1 'Pacific' No. 2543 *Melton* makes an imposing shot as it rounds the curve in effortless descent with a Down London Marylebone–Manchester express.

Gresley's class K3 2–6–0 No. 1154 coasts round the curve at Torside with an unidentified express in April 1940. The early haze has cleared to reveal Torside Reservoir below and patches of snow on the northern flank of Bleaklow Hill, one of Derbyshire's highest summits.

Midsummer 1940, and LNER class V2 2–6–2 No. 4830 sweeps through Torside with a Down London Marylebone–Manchester express. The distant iron foot-bridge spanning the tracks is at Torside level crossing where the post-war long distance footpath 'The Pennine Way' heads north to cross from Derbyshire into Cheshire by the dam of Torside Reservoir..

Following the V2, but at the very careful and leisurely pace of the heavy coal trains, a Robinson 2–8–0 LNER class O4 blows off steam as it passes the upper quadrant signal on the descent.

LNER class C1 'Atlantic' No. 4412 pounds across Torside level crossing with a Liverpool–Hull express. The front 'Barnum' coach with brass handrails less ornate than usual, is well patronized. The sheeting on the roof of No. 4412 to hide the firebox glare from enemy aircraft and the white painted buffer stop were purely wartime measures. A look-out man surveys the scene as the permanent way gang assemble their trolley in the foreground. None of them notice the photographer lurking behind the adjacent gritstone wall.

Wartime operating requirements could humble even the mightiest express locomotives. Here Gresley's pioneer Great Northern 'Pacific' No. 4470 *Great Northern*, covered in grime, passes Crowden with a Down goods. Some distance behind the engine is the dam supporting Woodhead Reservoir, the frozen surface of which was crossed during a wartime wintry spell by a party of soldiers who thought that they were walking over level fields to reach the George and Dragon situated on the far side in Cheshire. The moorlands to the north of the reservoir climb to the summit of Black Hill, the highest point in Cheshire.

Great Northern 0–6–0 class J2, one of only ten of the superheated version of Ivatt's J1 built by Gresley in 1912, trundles with a mixed freight on the Down slow line approaching Torside. The woodland above the railway boundary wall harboured many dead or dying and stunted trees suffering from the acid rain that fell from the long polluted atmosphere generated by a girdle of industrial towns. Only when the wind blew directly from the north, where there was nothing but the expansive Pennine moorland, was the air clear and visibility good. The walls and buildings were darkened by the deposit of soot and even the sheep were blackened by the 'moorland grime'. The old building above the track was registered on the map as a 'paper mill'.

LNER B17 4–6–0 'Footballer' No. 2864 *Liverpool* roars past the signals adjacent to Crowden station on a bleak Pennine day. The water column between the two up tracks enabled engines from either side to take water as necessary although it normally served only the slow line where trains were frequently brought to a halt until the main line was clear.

LNER class D11 4–4–0 No. 5501 *Mons*, one of the new series 'Directors', makes good headway with an Up Manchester–Cleethorpes express at Crowden. Immediately beyond the station the line followed the edge of the Woodhead Reservoir before the final approach to Woodhead Tunnel.

LNER class A1 'Pacific' No. 4473 *Solario* coasts towards the entrance of Woodhead Tunnel with the Up Marylebone express. Photographs of the tunnel were not attempted at this time as an armed guard at the tunnel mouth signified it as an important military objective.

As wartime security arrangements prevented the author from photographing the climax of the Woodhead line, the tunnels, it seems appropriate to include a small selection of post-war pictures to complete the record of the line.

Sporting the new British Railways number on the smokebox door, former LNER 2–6–0 class K3 emerges from the Down Woodhead Tunnel as No. 61978 with a Sheffield–Manchester express in April 1949. The rarely used station at Woodhead was notable because of the castle-like appearance of the solid gritstone station-master's house which matched the castellated ornamentations of the tunnel's prestigious façade. The bridge immediately in front of the train spanned the River Etherow and marked the boundary between Cheshire and Derbyshire. The station and Station House were in Derbyshire and the railway cottages, perched high above the rock face of the tunnel mouth, in Cheshire. The cottages were connected to the station by a very steep footpath following the topside of the gritstone wall. At the time of this photograph work had just commenced on the building of the new tunnel.

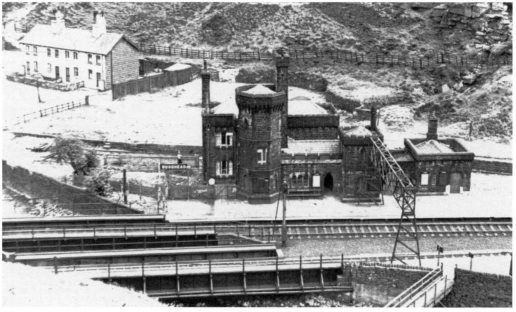

Woodhead station with the station-master's house forming part of the main building and other railway cottages in the background. The photograph was taken by Eric Oldham in December 1945 after a light fall of snow.

Sundays at Woodhead frequently meant single line working as essential tunnel repairs were carried out, the eastbound trains having to cross over at the station to take the Down tunnel up to Dunford Bridge. An unusual four-wheeled van blocks the Up line at the tunnel entrance. It has a clearance gauge rail fitted to the rear end and at the front has what appear to be observation windows on either side of a lamp. Two unidentified Thompson class B1 4–6–0s negotiate the crossover to the Down line as they doublehead the Sheffield-bound express about to enter the tunnel. Local gritstone used in the construction of the castle-like station building accentuates Woodhead's formidable landscape features. The distant water tank is brim full, as might be expected as the adjacent moorlands have an annual rainfall which reaches 60 in. These gathering grounds provide the River Etherow with its never ceasing flow, supplying Manchester's succession of reservoirs through Longdendale to Tintwistle.

Thompson's two-cylinder class B1 4–6–0 has been immaculately groomed for the honour of hauling the last steam train through the old Woodhead Tunnel on 3 June 1954. Alongside is the VIP
special headed by an electric locomotive to initiate the opening of the new tunnel. The author, a
teacher at Longdendale Secondary Modern School in Hollingworth at the time, persuaded the
head that the school should witness the opening ceremony and the whole school was transported
by coaches to the heights above the tunnel mouth to observe the historic occasion.

As the VIPs gather for the official pronouncements flag-bedecked Bo+Bo locomotive No. 26020
stands by in readiness to take the party through the tunnel, breaking the tape across the entrance
as part of the opening ceremony. In the foreground lie the tracks to and from the old twin bore tunnels. The fortress station buildings and platform have been swept away. A new and imposing
station-master's house is set well back and a little apart from the railway cottages.

Television crews film the opening ceremony from a specially constructed gantry as the VIPs listen to the Minister of Transport. As soon as they were back on board, the EM1 Bo+Bo No. 26020 slowly accelerated to break the tape and take the first passenger train through the new Woodhead Tunnel. Appropriately, the last coach of the train was the ex-LNER Coronation beaver tail observation coach, a fitting tribute to Gresley's masterpiece described at the outset of this work. In the background stands the massive water tank that originally supplied the steam locomotives. The tank was removed shortly afterwards, along with the tracks to the steam tunnels. In contrast to the old single bore smoke-filled atmosphere of the twin tunnels, the new twin track tunnel was cement lined and had electric lighting throughout.

Massive 'Supergrid' electricity pylons, capable of carrying 400,000 volts, now dominate the Woodhead Tunnel area as the Central Electricity Generating Board needed to cross the Pennines with a double-circuit line from Stalybridge to Doncaster. Objections to the routing of the huge pylons across the high moors led to the cables being taken underground through the old up steam tunnel. The rough lining of masonry had to be cleared of massive deposits of soot, up to 9 in thick in places, before the regrouting could be undertaken. As the cables required a water cooling system they were laid in a continuous running water conduit which could dissipate the heat. This cable troughing can be seen to the right along the line of the original steam track into the tunnel. The second pylon stands on the site of the approach loops. Only the remnants of the station platform remain. The buildings, signal-box and water tank have been swept away. Station House remains like some large country estate residence standing in its own grounds, but its state is betrayed by the immediate foreground that has an air of neglect and sterility.

The diversion of passenger traffic on to other trans-Pennine routes in the early seventies left only freight trains to maintain a service on the Woodhead line until financial problems and the recession in the early eighties caused further reduction in traffic and eventually led to the closure of the line in July 1981. The desolate nature apparent today is a reminder of the harsh reality of this place, but the harshest reality lies in its history. The line and its original tunnels were built by an army of labourers in utterly wretched conditions and at an appalling price of human misery, but they provided an essential link across the Pennines that lasted for a hundred years. The new tunnel, which should have considerably extended this service, had an operational life of less than thirty years. Apart from the financial aspect, the three tunnels had cost some sixty-seven lives and caused a massive toll of injuries. After such a heavy price one can only grieve that the line is no more. May this collection of wartime photographs keep alive the memory of those who served this north-west community so well and for so long.

CHAPTER THREE

EXPLOITS OF A MOBILE PHOTOGRAPHER

By late 1940 the war was beginning to take hold more severely. Station photography was no longer practical, except by very discreet manoeuvres, and by now I was longing to record the activity on the east and west coast main lines. These potential problems were resolved by the purchase of my bicycle, a boost to transport facilities which inevitably led to wider horizons. For the first time in my life I was independently and completely mobile. At an average speed of 15 m.p.h., it was a simple matter to calculate the possibilities. The LMS main line near Warrington could be reached in about two-and-a-half hours and Tickhill, near Doncaster, in just under four hours. Tickhill was only about four miles from the LNER main line at Bawtry and the relatively new Youth Hostels Association had a hostel there. I joined the association as a means to that end. By cycling after work on the Friday, I could reach the hostel before 9 p.m. and could spend the whole of Saturday and until tea-time on the Sunday by the line-side before returning home. The overnight cost, if memory serves correct, was 2s. (10p), inclusive of breakfast and packed lunch, and an evening dinner was offered at an equally reasonable price. All this fitted within a fairly tight budget, but the problems of cycling in the blackout made the start of any venture inevitably hesitant; the visits were put into abeyance pending the onset of spring and the lighter evenings. By midsummer, with the imposition of double summer time, two hours ahead of GMT, it was light until amost midnight!

It was my normal practice to work overtime operating the firm's telephone switchboard for a couple of hours each evening as this enhanced my weekly income to about one guinea (£1.05). It also gave me access to a typewriter which was helpful in typing the information relating to a few photographs of the Woodhead line that I had enlarged and wished to despatch to *Railways*. I was much impressed by the quality of the layout and the reproduction of photographs in the magazine and was delighted when two of my prints were reproduced in the March 1941 edition.

The captions were suitably vague and undated as was the custom during the war. The previous November, the magazine had commented on this matter:

Several readers have written during the last few months saying that the lack of place-names in some of the illustration captions irritates them. We quite agree that such descriptions as 'at an East Coast terminus' or 'on the main line in Blankshire', are extremely vague, but it has to be. The censors have the final say in these matters.

The following month another notch of security was tightened as the magazine commented that 'we have been requested by the censor to refrain from publishing detailed particulars of locomotive stock changes of the four main line railways.'

Notwithstanding, in April 1941 the magazine commented on the Southern Railway's first 'Pacific' built to a new design and also referred to the LNER's new lightweight 2–6–2, 'Bantam Cock', the last of Sir Nigel Gresley's designs. Sadly, he died early in that same month.

A double standard appeared to have emerged on the photographic front as was confirmed by a very ambiguous statement in *Railways*:

There is no law against taking pictures of moving trains but anyone seen using a camera in the neighbourhood of a railway is certainly liable to make himself suspect.

The war situation was deteriorating by this time which obviously wasn't helping. During April we were retreating before Rommel in North Africa and the Germans invaded Yugoslavia and Greece. Britain had suffered directly from the blitz, but none of this could be recorded by the amateur photographer. The cycle rides to Tickhill took me through Sheffield which, like Manchester and many other cities, had been transformed by the aerial bombardment. Whole areas had been laid waste and the road meandered among great piles of rubble and the skeletal remains of former buildings. Route finding was a problem as all road signposts had been removed. Map reading in the countryside offered no great difficulties but within the ruined format of a city it was very perplexing and my initial route finding was based more on conversations with the people I met. Subsequent journeys were no problem as the ruins were recognizably unchanged. By summer 1941 the worst of the blitz in northern England was over.

Tickhill Youth Hostel was remote from the village and primitive by modern standards. I undertook to do my 'hostel duty' early by bringing in the necessary buckets of water from the well at the bottom of the garden, there being no other supply. This enabled me to leave early for my day's photography at the lineside and I found a remote farm crossing where I spent many hours undisturbed on these weekend photographic missions.

In the constant search for new viewpoints towards the end of May 1941 I cycled to a bridge which carried the Great North Road (the original A1) across the tracks. Below it was a reasonably good position that offered some variety. I chained my bicycle to a wooden fence at the side of the bridge and scrambled down the bank and a little way along the track to my chosen vantage point. As I scanned the track in both directions my attention was drawn to the peaked cap and peculiar antics of a man on the bridge. Every time I looked in his direction, he ducked out of sight. An A4 passed on an Up express and was followed shortly by another but I did not dare take a shot because of that ever watchful eye. It didn't take much imagination to know what the man was thinking. I decided to cut my losses and find another place. As I climbed over the fence to retrieve my bike the special constable approached, adjusting his peaked cap as he came towards me.

'And what do you think you've been up to?' he queried as I unlocked the chain that secured my bike which had obviously betrayed my presence. With a camera dangling round my neck I thought that it seemed pretty obvious what I had been up to. The man had to be humoured though and I perceived that my response would be crucial.

'I was going to photograph the trains but when I saw you watching me I thought that I had better find some other place.'

'Don't you know there's a war on?' he said firmly. 'That is the main line to Scotland and this is the Great North Road. They are both military objectives so I must now arrest you on suspicion.'

With that he escorted me along the road to the local police station, a small detached house with a jail cell for a back room. Unlike the youth hostel there was no rule about staying out until after five. Accommodation was free, there were no chores and it was less than a mile from the main line. There were distinct possibilities but these were ruled out as there was no view from the window!

Quick thinking was obviously required if I was to avoid being detained. My identity card, the small buff card that every adult carried, not only gave all my details but confirmed that I was in the LDV, the Local Defence Volunteers, a citizen's army that was formed to defend the realm in the dark days when the German invasion seemed imminent. That proved that I wasn't a spy and that, in fact, the reverse was true – I was actively engaged against the enemy as a member of this early version of the Home Guard ('Dad's Army').

'You don't look old enough to be in the LDV,' said the sergeant.

'I'm seventeen,' I replied, 'and I'm going to volunteer for the RAF as a photographer.'

There was little doubt that this information saved me from an unwanted residential stay. After due warning that both the A1 road and the railway were both important military objectives, 'not to mention the bridge', I was further cautioned and then allowed to leave.

The special constable left the station with me and for a short while tailed me on his bike, but younger legs soon carried me out of sight and, with quick avoiding action down an old farm track, I returned to the tiny remote crossing where I continued the good work. I had lost some precious hours on a glorious summer's day. Acknowledging waves and broad smiles were given to drivers to reassure them whose side I was on as I took my last few photographs. Time was short. I would soon have to start the long cycle journey home.

The final photographic mission in 1941 was a cycling tour planned to follow the LNER main line north of Doncaster to Darlington, across Stainmore to Penrith and thence by the LMS main line south to Hest Bank. As a junior cost clerk only one week's holiday was allowed, but with a weekend at either end I had a ten-day span and started with the short run to Castleton in Derbyshire on the Friday evening, about 11 June. This shortened the distance to Sheffield and Doncaster on the following day to give that little extra lineside time. At Darlington on the Sunday evening, a spontaneous decision was made to catch a train to Edinburgh for a first visit to Scotland. Waverley was a superb setting but the weather was appalling. On the Monday, as I photographed the line from the foot-bridges in Princes Street Gardens, the rain was almost continuous, but the camera managed to cope and produced reasonable pictures of the events.

The most astonishing arrival was that of an American 2–8–0, one of the first built to a simple design suiting our loading gauge and sent over to Britain under the 'Lease-Lend' agreement. Not until December 1942 was any mention made of these locomotives in the railway press, and then just a brief comment that some American 2–8–0 locomotives had been shipped over to this country for general use and that people had noted a 'new sounding whistle'. In January 1943 more details were forthcoming, which confirmed that the first batch had arrived in 1941 and added that they had required some adjustment before they could be put into traffic. The article stated that three USA locomotives were hauling trains between the Glasgow district and the 'Kingdom of Fife' and had not given any trouble in service.

The two photographs that I took of USA locomotive No. 1834 were promptly despatched to *Railways* on my return home in June 1941. The editor, G.H. Lake, was delighted, but it was not until October 1944, over three years after the photographs had been submitted, that the pictures eventually appeared in the magazine. The censor had evidently relaxed the code as by that time the conduct of the war had turned very much in our favour.

The rest of my cycling tour was enhanced by the almost continuous sunshine and the highlight proved to be the exceptional day spent at Scout Green level crossing near Shap and the magnificent run through the Lune Gorge, in those days totally unspoiled by motorways or even the sound of road traffic. Petrol rationing ensured that the wartime road traffic was minimal. This made cycling a sheer delight and considerably enhanced the enjoyment of the tour.

The kind reception that I had received from the crossing keepers at Scout Green was acknowledged on my next fleeting visit, this time as a member of the forces. I had joined the RAFVR in 1942 and in October 1943 travelled aboard a special train with a contingent of young airmen bound for a navigation course in Canada. The *Queen Elizabeth* lay off Gourock in the Firth of Clyde awaiting our arrival to transport us across the Atlantic to New York. As we passed over Shap in the early hours I waved furiously to attract the attention of the crossing keeper and threw out a postcard as we sped by. No doubt he thought that it would be a message for home but it was one of the photographs of an LMS streamlined 'Pacific' on the climb approaching the Scout Green Cabin that I had taken just over two years earlier. Before we rounded the curve I saw the keeper pick up the card and wave in response. I sat back feeling pleased at this momentary contact.

The war situation had considerably improved by 1943 after the very heavy set-backs culminating with the Japanese attack on Pearl Harbour in December 1941 and their expansion across the Pacific from New Guinea to the very borders of India. In the meantime, there had been some changes in railway practice.

From July 1941 the Southern Railway declared that, for reasons of economy, all mixed traffic, goods and older types of passenger engines were to be painted black, unlined, although light green livery would still be permitted on selected classes of main line passenger locomotives such as the new 'Pacifics', the 'Lord Nelsons' and other similar engines. By January 1942 several LNER streamlined A4 'Pacifics' had passed through the shops and were running black and unlined. Instructions had been given that all LNER locomotives were to be treated thus, and were to have the new style lettering 'NE' replacing the former 'LNER' on the tender. Even more startling, the streamlined aerofoil skirting had been removed from the sides of the streamlined 'Pacifics' to facilitate maintenance. This made the whole of the motion more easily accessible. It also revealed for the first time the full splendour of the motion and in that respect transformed the whole appearance of the locomotives. The chime whistles were removed and replaced by normal whistles as 'someone' had complained that the chime was too similar to the air-raid sirens. Just how the one minute statutory wailing of a siren could be confused with the brief and melodious chime of an A4 seems beyond comprehension but the change still went ahead. Thompsons' reputed dislike of Gresley's inspired creations may possibly have clinched the matter.

The threat of massive air raids diminished considerably after the *Luftwaffe* moved east to attack Russia, and in February 1942 stations were permitted to have 'controlled beam' lighting for station platforms. As the threat of invasion also receded after 1941 place-names and road signs were reinstated. My cycle tour had relied almost entirely upon map reading. The difficulties that road users without the appropriate maps encountered on longer journeys ensured the rapid restoration of the appropriate signposts when the order was rescinded.

Despite this improvement April 1942 saw the initiation of the notorious 'Baedeker 3 star raids', the Germans adopting this rating from a famous tourist guide and applying it to those towns or cities selected for attack as reprisal raids after RAF attacks on Germany. They bombed picturesque and historic cities such as Exeter, Bath and Norwich. York was attacked on the night of 28/29 April and on this occasion a military objective, the railway station, was hit and badly damaged. A train within it was destroyed and, nearby, Gresley's streamlined A4 'Pacific' No. 4469 *Sir Ralph Wedgwood* received a direct hit and the locomotive was later scrapped as beyond repair.

The railway press continued to issue periodic warnings. The March 1942 edition of *Railways* stated:

> We would like to remind those readers who take notes and make observations at stations to be very careful in their methods and actions, and not to act in a manner as to cause suspicion and thus give the police and station staffs a lot of unnecessary trouble.

The magazine underlined that warning with a second in November of that year:

> On no account can photographs be taken on the railway companies' premises. Pictures can be taken from adjoining property, but the photographer will be in trouble if the view should contain anything of a military nature. As all railways are very important things from a military point of view, and also as many trains are run solely for military purposes, we advise against the taking of any photographs during the present emergency.

Here was a comforting ambiguity that left a tiny loophole for the committed!

I had already received considerable encouragement as the July edition of *Railways* had published several of my wartime photographs in support of an article written by my brother, Eric, and entitled 'Recent Locomotive Working on the Sheffield–Manchester Line, LNER'. This great incentive would normally have impelled me to produce a follow-up but my photographic sorties were suddenly restricted because of other commitments.

I had already volunteered at the age of seventeen to join the RAFVR as a photographer and was invited to attend for interview shortly after my eighteenth birthday in October 1941. Not having the commercial background I was rejected but a local photographer and friend, Jim Drinkwater, offered to instruct me in all the techniques and processes involved in commercial work. Nightly evening sessions, overtime at the engineering firm's telephone switchboard and full day Saturday sessions, together with Home Guard duties, left little time for my railway pursuits.

When I next applied there were no vacancies for photographers and I opted for air-crew training for which I was accepted. I was then required to transfer to Hyde's Home Guard HQ signalling unit and to attend the Air Training Corps in preparation for my service life. On 5 October 1942, immediately following my nineteenth birthday, I travelled by warrant to the RAFVR reception centre at St John's Wood, London. I chose the

LNER Manchester to Marylebone route and was hauled by an old favourite, Class A1 'Pacific' No. 2558 *Tracery* on the most enjoyable six-and-a-half hour journey over the familiar ground by Woodhead to Sheffield and thence south to Marylebone. What better way to start one's wartime service in the forces!

The wartime traffic on the railways was considerably heavier than in pre-war days. On the LMS alone in 1942 loaded wagon miles totalled 1,713 million, an increase of 34 per cent on pre-war years, and involved the weekly use of some 390,000 wagons to move the traffic originating on the LMS. Their locomotives covered 121 million miles hauling freight trains (nearly 19 million more than in 1938), and 55 million more passenger journeys were made in 1942 than in the previous year, and these were classified as 'necessary' journeys comprising increased services and workmen's travel – a total increase of nearly 50 million journeys above the comparative peacetime figure. That was the measure of the workload. Nearly 500 special trains, passengers and freight, ran weekly on behalf of the services and, in addition, between 800 and 900 parties of forces personnel were accommodated each week on ordinary timetabled trains. All of this was quite apart from the large numbers who travelled without reserving accommodation, the many thousands going to or from home on leave or transferring to other units. Of some 27,000 trains run each day by the LMS, 17,000 were freight moving 3 million tons of munitions and merchandise daily.

The LNER fulfilled an equally significant role in serving its country, giving much satisfaction to traffic control with many 'troop specials' operating when the pressure of normal daily traffic was extremely heavy. The big engines of the Gresley era more than matched the demands with many trains comprising more than twenty coaches. The class W1 4–6–4 streamlined locomotive No. 10000 was observed passing through Doncaster with an up express of no less than twenty-six coaches. Many of the timetabled passenger trains had to be duplicated, such was the demand for transport.

A further, if somewhat incidental, illustration of the railways' contribution to the war effort is demonstrated by the amount of pasteboard made from the used tickets collected by both the LMS and LNE Railways. In 1942 alone just over 262 million tickets added no less than 222 tons of pasteboard to the salvage campaign.

Everyone had to play their part. The slogan 'Is your journey really necessary?' was continually publicized by the very organizations that would be trying to tempt people to travel in normal times. Official notices stated: Every unnecessary journey, every hour's delay in loading or unloading a wagon is a definite disservice to the national effort, and a postponement of the day of final victory. Each individual act of thoughtlessness or selfishness may seem too insignificant to matter, but in a huge nation-wide organisation, the cumulative effect is tremendous – thus were we exhorted, every one of us, to play our part.

In busy times 95 per cent of all wagons were in circulation. Train loads had increased in size, many trains were duplicated and engines were kept out on the road for long periods of running with little time for servicing them in the running sheds. It followed that there should be some deterioration.

In March 1943 W. Lees reported in *Railways* that after five days' scrutiny on the LMS main line, only four engines matched the pre-war standard for cleanliness. All other locomotives were thickly coated with a sooty layer, a symptom of the unremitting service appropriately dubbed 'austerity rust'. Not even the prestigious thoroughbreds, the streamlined and unstreamlined 'Pacifics' and a host of others, were spared. Numbers were often completely hidden beneath the grime despite the occasional wipe down to assist in the identity. The coaches matched the engines in this external filth. That such magnificent engines and stock should be reduced to such circumstances, rusted and uncared for, was an inescapable but sad reflection of the times.

Just one bright spark emerged and that was the survival of many old engines whose service life had long expired. Thickly coated with dust and oil, these 'Old Contemptibles' worked their stint along with the rest to help the war effort. It was a fine testimony to the workmanship and design that went into the building of these veterans that, after so many years, they were still able to give such admirable service.

The tide of war had turned. After Dunkirk, when there remained on British soil a total of only five hundred guns, many of which were museum pieces, and Churchill had rallied the nation with his 'we will never surrender' speech, it was decided that the church bells throughout the country would remain silent and would be rung only to give the nation an audible warning if the Germans invaded – an up-dated version of the beacon fires that once signalled the Armada. Hitler's plans to land twenty divisions on the south coast were foiled but the bells remained silent until 15 November 1942 when they were rung to celebrate the victory in Egypt that followed El Alamein.

By the end of 1944 the number of USA locomotives in Britain had steadily decreased since D-Day as large numbers of them were already on the Continent building up reserves behind the 'front'. The distinctive whistle had become a familiar feature in almost every part of Britain that was served by a main line railway, a fact that made the removal of the chime whistles off Gresley's streamlined A4 'Pacifics' seem even more incongruous.

One quote from a speech made by the chairman of the LMS deserves repeating:

The country as a whole is now reaping the benefit of a first class railway system which in pre-war days was built up and maintained by private enterprise in the face of strong competition and out-of-date legislation.

It seems appropriate to end this account of the railways in wartime Britain by quoting just one passage from an editorial in the February 1943 edition of *Railways*:

It should be the endeavour of all true railwaymen – professional or amateur enthusiasts – to foster this idea of a national railway museum, and to bring it into being before it is too late. Any scheme for a NRM must have the support of the main line companies if it is to be successful and to become a lasting benefit to posterity. From the railway companies' point of view, the propoganda and advertising value of the museum would be high indeed. Any capital expended upon forming and maintaining the collection would soon reap a dividend in the shape of increased interest in the railways and their history. Indeed, in the course of time, the museum could be self-supporting by means of a small charge for admission.

The late G.H. Lake's forecasting words bring us back to the present. My photography of railways in wartime ceased abruptly when my 'Purma' camera was stolen from a safe in Canada. After the war, a 16 mm cine camera took its place to record in colour and in sound the final years of steam from 1961. It only remains to transfer the film onto tape. Photography is a powerful medium for the sharing of experiences. I trust that this work will convey the atmosphere of the railways in wartime Britain.

THE EAST AND WEST COAST MAIN LINES

Work as a junior cost clerk at a local engineering firm prevented further mid-week photography from September 1940 but provided funds to purchase a second-hand bicycle which enabled the author to cycle to the west and east coast main lines at weekends. The former, being nearer, provided opportunities in April and May 1941 when it was possible to cycle the return route within the hours of daylight. Cycling during the blackout posed more hazards, this situation not helped by the author's poor night vision.

Lineside vantage points were located just south of Crewe, near Acton Bridge, and just north of Warrington at Winwick Quay. By late May and June the LNER main line south of Doncaster became accessible on weekend stays at Tickhill Youth Hostel. Junior staff at that time were only allowed one week's holiday but within this period a grand tour embracing both lines was accomplished.

In October 1941 the author was accepted by the RAFVR for aircrew training. Time and circumstances did not allow more than very brief photographic opportunities after that.

'Royal Scot' 4–6–0 class 7P No. 6114 *Coldstream Guardsman* heads south from Crewe with a train of empty stock. The limited cleaning has been restricted to the cabside number, half of which remains obscured by grime.

The West Coast Main Line in Cheshire and South Lancashire, 1941
LMS

Begrimed 'Patriot' class 6P5F 4–6–0 No. 5509 heads an Up wartime troop train south of Crewe. The identification number has been chalked on the smokebox door, a method frequently adopted by the LMS when printed cards were not available.

An unidentified former LNWR 0–8–0 class G2 locomotive with the round-topped firebox and LNWR chimney on an Up mixed freight just south of Crewe. The lineside photographic activity does not pass unnoticed from the footplate.

'Royal Scot' class 7P 4–6–0 No. 6149 *The Middlesex Regiment*, bearing the regimental crest above the name-plate, hauls an unusually short but unidentified express south of Crewe.

Stanier taper boiler 'Black Five' No. 5129 with an Up express to the south of Crewe as it overtakes the brake end of a mixed freight train on the slow line.

An unidentified 'Duchess', one of the five such locomotives of the 'Coronation' class 8P 4–6–2s which were built without the streamlining in 1938, on a Down express approaching Crewe.

LMS 'Royal Scot' class 7P 4–6–0 No. 6163 *Civil Service Rifleman* heads towards Crewe on a Down Manchester express in August 1941. An unidentified Up express and an Up goods which occupy adjacent tracks on either side are an indication of the heavy wartime traffic.

LMS 'Princess' class 8P 4–6–2 No. 6201 *Princess Elizabeth* at speed on an Up express to the south of Crewe in the late summer of 1941.

An unidentified LMS 'Patriot' class 6P5F 4–6–0 with a Down troop train approaching Crewe, summer 1941.

LMS 'Jubilee' class 6P5F 4–6–0 No. 5638 *Zanzibar* with an unidentified Down express at Acton Bridge.

LMS 'Patriot' class 6P5F 4–6–0 No. 5523 *Bangor* on a Down fitted freight train at Acton Bridge.

LMS 'Royal Scot' class 7P 4–6–0 No. 6163 *Civil Service Rifleman* on the Down London–Manchester express at Acton Bridge.

An unidentified LMS 'Jubilee' class 6P5F 4–6–0 at Acton Bridge with a stopping train of mixed stock.

An unidentified streamlined 'Coronation' class 8P 4–6–2 in begrimed maroon livery on a Down London–Glasgow express at Acton Bridge.

One of three surviving Midland unsuperheated 4–4–0s built in 1888 and rebuilt in 1910, No. 383 pilots an unidentified LMS 'Jubilee' on a Down express at Acton Bridge.

The Main Line at Winwick Quay, North of Warrington, April/May 1941
LMSR

Black paint on the upper half of the goods yard lamp ensured that the light was directed downwards to meet the stringent blackout regulations. LMS class 5 4–6–0 No. 5312, one of Stanier's taper boiler designs better known as 'Black Fives', approaches Warrington with an Up express. The footpath which crossed the line by the lattice girder bridge provided other vantage points from which to photograph the line at Winwick Quay.

An unidentified 'Royal Scot' on a Down express viewed from the Winwick Quay foot-bridge as it passes an Up goods trundling to the south.

A Down London Euston–Glasgow express hauled by one of the original five streamlined 'Coronation' class 8P 4–6–2s sporting the blue livery which initiated their service on the 'Coronation Scot'.

Troop trains carried their identification numbers on a card attached to the smokebox door. On the LMS it was normally prefixed by the letter 'W' which might be interpreted as the 'War Department' but was probably a route reference to the west coast main line. 'Royal Scot' class 7P 4–6–0 No. 6125 displays this code as it coasts through Winwick Quay with a troop train heading south. The name-plate and crest of *3rd Carabinier* replaced the locomotive's former name, *Lancashire Witch*. Twenty-five of this class were originally named after early locomotives and later altered to accommodate the names of further regiments.

LMS 'Jubilee' class 6P5F 4–6–0 No. 5657 *Tyrwhitt* reversing along the southbound main line as a light engine but still carrying the W632 identity card attached to the smokebox door. The driver views the lineside photographer with some apprehension.

A cheery wave and smile from the footplate indicate a different response from LMS 'Jubilee 'class 6P5F 4–6–0 No. 5628 *Somaliland* as it glides past in immaculate condition.

An unidentified 'Royal Scot' class 7P 4–6–0 pilots a 'Black Five' at the head of a Down troop special as it speeds past a new vantage point near St Helens Canal at Winwick Quay.

LMS 'Royal Scot' class 7P 4–6–0 No. 6132 *The King's Regiment Liverpool* rumbles past with a Down express, its exhaust invisible in the warmth of a sunny day in late April 1941.

One of the later series of streamlined 'Coronation Pacifics', class 8P No. 6236 *City of Bradford*, looking splendid in its standard LMS maroon and gold livery on a Down express from London to Glasgow.

A veteran of fifty years, ex-LNWR 2–4–2T No. 6832 on extended lease for war service, heads north from Warrington in a sprightly manner with the lightweight Earlestown push-and-pull.

111

LMS 'Royal Scot' class 7P 4–6–0 No. 6102 *Black Watch* working well on a Down express for Glasgow as it passes Winwick Quay.

Another veteran ex-LNWR engine, an unidentified 'Precursor' class 4–4–0, hurries past with a short express train of old Midland stock heading for Manchester from North Wales. One of 130 locomotives of this type built between 1904 and 1907 and later rebuilt with superheater and Belpaire firebox, it was among many such engines retained past their normal life expectancy for war service.

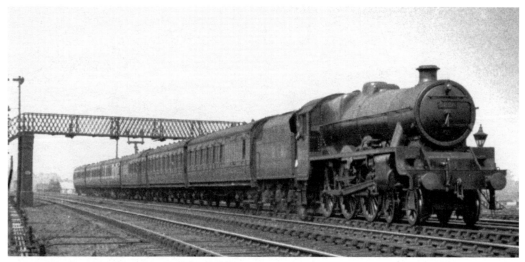

LMS 'Jubilee' class 6P5F 4–6–0 No. 5626 *Seychelles* in immaculate condition as it steams towards Warrington with a stopping train.

'Coronation' class 8P 4–6–2 No. 6230 *Duchess of Buccleuch*, the first of the five 'Pacifics' to be built without the streamlining in 1938, heads south through Winwick Quay with an Up Glasgow–London express.

An unidentified LMS mixed traffic 4–6–0 class 5 ('Black Five') hauling a troop train overtakes sister engine No. 5427 on a mineral train as they both head south through Winwick Quay.

Another life-extended 'Precursor' class 4–4–0 with a light stopping train from North Wales to Manchester.

An unidentified GWR 4–6–0 'Hall' class, one of Collet's two-cylinder general-purpose express loco-motives with 6 ft driving wheels, joins the varied assortment of traffic with an express from Chester to Manchester.

Streamlined 'Coronation' class 8P 4–6–2 No. 6236 *City of Bradford* speeds a troop train northwards through Winwick Quay. The engine displays the standard LMS maroon livery with the enhancing V-shaped sweep of the curving bands of gold which accentuates the streamlined shape and continues along the line of the boiler and across the tender.

'Coronation' class 8P non-streamlined 'Pacific' No. 6230 *Duchess of Buccleuch* makes a fast run through Winwick Quay with a Down London–Glasgow express on a warm day early in May 1941.

'Princess' class 8P 4–6–2 No. 6200 *The Princess Royal*, the first of the LMS 'Pacifics' built in 1933 but with the larger tender fitted later, shows itself to be in excellent trim as it speeds past on an Up Glasgow–London express after twenty months of war service.

LMS 'Patriot' 4–6–0 class 6P5F No. 5541 *Duke of Sutherland* speeds another troop train south through Winwick Quay.

'Coronation' class 8P non-streamlined 'Pacific' No. 6232 *Duchess of Montrose* provides the final shot at Winwick Quay as it sweeps past the signal-box with a lengthy southbound express. Two Gresley coaches at the front of the train, one of them a brake third, make a contrast with the remainder of the coaches which are standard LMS stock.

The East Coast Main Line South of Doncaster, 1941
LNER

LNER A4 streamlined 'Pacific' No. 4466 *Herring Gull*, begrimed but running well, speeds through Ranskill with an Up express from Leeds to London King's Cross in the cool and slightly misty air of early morning at the end of May 1941.

Ivatt's Great Northern 4–4–0 design class D2 No. 4377 heads a mixed freight at a steady pace through the level pastures at Ranskill.

A brilliant day in early June 1941 gave a rare opportunity to use the focal plane shutter of the 'Purma Special' camera at its fast speed of 1/450 second. Gresley's streamlined 'Pacific' class A4 No. 4467 *Wild Swan* gleamed in the mid-day sun as the express hurled past at a speed which must have exceeded the officially approved wartime maximum of 60 m.p.h. The mid-day sun may have been bright, but the main frame of the locomotive with the side aerofoils cast a heavy shadow over the wheels.

One of Gresley's 5 ft 8 in three-cylinder 2–6–0 mixed traffic class K3 engines No. 2936 joins the procession of freight trains heading south through Ranskill. The large boiler and imposing steam pipes add to the impressive appearance of these locomotives.

A new vantage point from a lonely farm track crossing near Ranskill provides another early morning setting as LNER 2–6–2 class V2 No. 4874 heads to the north with a Down mixed goods.

LNER class A1 'Pacific' No. 4476 *Royal Lancer* looking well groomed as it heads this Down stopping train towards Doncaster.

A changed viewpoint from the opposite side of the farm crossing gives a new angle as a Gresley 2–6–2 class V2 No. 4846 speeds northwards with another unmarked express. Following Dunkirk destination boards were removed from trains as part of the policy of removing all place-names to confuse the enemy should they manage to land.

The fast approach of two locomotives, light engines in tandem, forced the photographer to make a sudden decision and take a close shot of the leading engine, A1 'Pacific' No. 2564 *Knight of the Thistle*. The choice was immediately regretted as the second locomotive turned out to be none other than that renowned 'Scot', the P2 class 2–8–2 No. 2004 *Mons Meg*. From the state of the locomotives they were returning from a running-in turn after overhaul at Doncaster prior to them undertaking normal duties. A position well back in the fields would have made a better record of this one-off opportunity.

LNER class A1 'Pacific' No. 4477 *Gay Crusader* with a lengthy Down express of twenty-three coaches. Many of these wartime expresses were of such length that it became customary to count the coaches as they passed and on one occasion, at Doncaster, the 4–6–4 class W1 No. 10000 was observed at speed with an extraordinary load of twenty-six coaches on an Up express. Destinations of the trains were often obscure as only a few carried destination boards, apparently in contravention of the wartime regulations.

A new location near Bawtry with a background of loose coupled wagons offered an alternative range of viewpoints. In apple green livery class C7 'Atlantic' No. 735, a North Eastern 4–4–2 of Raven design with a modified tender from class Q6, makes a rare appearance south of Doncaster as it backs down light engine towards Retford.

LNER class V2 2–6–2 No. 4843 *King's Own Yorkshire Light Infantry*, one of only seven 'Green Arrows' named before the war, makes a spirited run past with an unidentified Down express.

LNER class A3 'Pacific' No. 2751 *Humorist* and the Down King's Cross–Leeds express were well groomed even after twenty months of war service. This locomotive was fitted with a double blast pipe in 1937 but the drivers complained that the smoke frequently drifted down to obscure their view and this led to further alterations in the following January. The beading was removed from the chimney and small wing deflector plates were fitted alongside the double chimney. This resolved the problem and the alterations were retained.

LNER 2–6–2 class V2 No. 4823 races past with a Down mixed freight train heading for Doncaster.

North Eastern class Q5 two-cylinder 0–8–0 No. 2129 makes steady progress with a Down freight train on a hot sunny afternoon that fails to hide the deep exhaust.

Rising mists surround the next morning's first shot as A1 'Pacific' No. 4481 *St Simon* speeds north with a Down unmarked express.

The world record breaker for steam traction, LNER streamlined A4 'Pacific' No. 4468 *Mallard*, follows *St Simon* in the early morning procession. The plaque which recorded the record 126 m.p.h. was not fixed to the streamlined casing until after the war. The large double chimney was not as aesthetic in appearance as the single type but it considerably enhanced the performance of the engines.

A second double chimney A4 'Pacific' No. 4903 *Peregrine* follows *Mallard* in the morning procession of Down express trains. Half of the double chimney A4s thus passed within a half-hour of each other on that morning.

At a slower pace another vintage Great Northern design, class D2 4–4–0 No. 4390, leaks steam as it hauls a Down freight towards Doncaster. After taking this picture the author searched for a new location and was arrested at the new site before a single picture had been taken.

Released after interrogation at the local police station near Bawtry, a swift return to the remote farm track level crossing at Ranskill, well away from prying eyes, secured this shot of A4 'Pacific' No. 4499 *Sir Murrough Wilson* heading north with a Down King's Cross–Edinburgh express. This locomotive, named to honour a director, was one of the few embellished with a stainless steel lower rim to the side valances and cut out stainless steel numbers and letters on the cab and tender.

The final shot at Ranskill as Gresley 2–6–2 class V2 No. 4843 *King's Own Yorkshire Light Infantry*, still immaculate, whistles over the farm track level crossing with a Down express, unmarked but probably for Leeds. The Up line signals indicate that another train is approaching, a frequent occurrence emphasizing the high level of activity on the line.

THE GRAND TOUR, 6 – 14 JUNE 1941

A photographic record of the wartime railways on a cycle tour arranged to follow the LNER main line northwards from near Doncaster and the LMS main line from Penrith to Hest Bank, near Carnforth.

DATE	ITINERARY
6 Friday evening	Cycle from Hyde to Castleton Youth Hostel.
7 Saturday	Cycle from Castleton via Sheffield to Tickhill Youth Hostel. Brief photography at Ranskill.
8 Sunday	Cycle on route to follow the main line via Doncaster, Selby and York to Darlington. By train to Edinburgh.
9 Monday	Photography from Princes Street Gardens.
10 Tuesday	By train to Darlington. Cycle over Stainmore to Penrith. Follow the LMS main line to Shap. Youth Hostel Swindale Beck (2 nights).
11 Wednesday	Day at the lineside at Scout Green Signal Cabin.
12 Thursday	Cycle to Scout Green and thence via Tebay, Dillicar and Lowgill to Hest Bank. To Long Preston Youth Hostel for the night.
13 Friday	Cycle via Clitheroe and Preston to Liverpool and via the Mersey Tunnel to the Wirral and North Wales. Abergele Youth Hostel.
14 Saturday	Cycle via Chester to home (Hyde).

The last of the series of thirty-five streamlined A4 'Pacifics' of the LNER, No. 4903 *Peregrine*, was built in July 1938 and was one of only four of this class to be fitted with a double chimney at that time. Varied combinations of rolling stock made up the wartime expresses and this mixture of vintage clerestory with standard Gresley coaches and an articulated twin green and cream tourist buffet unit was typical. The loads were frequently extremely heavy on this line and the trains often exceeded twenty coaches.

The East Coast Main Line
LNER

An unidentified 4–4–2, one of Ivatt's large boilered Great Northern 'Atlantics', makes a moderate pace with a mixed freight on the Up LNER main line near Ranskill. The two outside cylinders, large 6 ft 8 in driving wheels and the wide firebox were characteristics of this Gresley improved locomotive and these very versatile engines often hauled major expresses such as the Pullmans and on at least two occasions took over the prestigious 'Silver Jubilee' streamlined express in rare emergencies.

A remote section of double track near Doncaster offered a view with a Great Northern somersault signal to the fore. Raven North Eastern 4–4–2 class 7 'Atlantic' No. 735 makes its second run past the camera within the month, piloting a very grimy and unidentified A1 'Pacific' on a Down express, and almost obscures the signal with its exhaust. A linesman, following the track, caused premature abandonment of this site.

A gentle curve south of Selby provides the setting for Gresley's D49 three-cylinder 4–4–0 'Hunt' class No. 288 *The Percy* on a Down stopping train of suburban stock.

Gresley A1 'Pacific' No. 2547 *Doncaster* with an Up Edinburgh–London King's Cross express of some twenty-one coaches in very good external condition even after twenty-one months of war service. Although the 'Flying Scotsman' express did not carry the famous headboards, a wartime restricted equivalent made the much slower journey and was frequently duplicated.

Gresley's 2–6–2 'Green Arrow' mixed traffic locomotives were designed for fast freight or passengers. Under wartime conditions V2 No. 4813 coasts round the Selby curve with the loosely coupled mineral wagons of an unfitted freight. Unlike some railway staff, this crew were happy to be photographed.

A bridge across the long straight and uncurving line north of York provides a suitable vantage point as a Raven North Eastern 'Atlantic' 4–4–2 class C7 No. 718, built by the North British Loco Co. in 1911, makes good progress with an Up mixed freight train. The tender of the locomotive formerly belonged to a North Eastern class Q6 0–8–0 mineral engine No. 2223 and was transferred to this locomotive in 1933 following suggestions by a York driver about the advantages of such a move. The authorities adopted the idea and carried it out.

LNER 2–6–2 class V2 No. 4831 *Durham School* was one of the few of this class of locomotive to be named, the ceremony having been performed on 15 June 1939, almost exactly two years before this photograph was taken. Drifting smoke caused by a strong easterly wind partially obscures the Gresley coaches on this Up express.

The first of Gresley's 'Pacifics', A1 No. 4470 *Great Northern*, south of Darlington with an Up express for King's Cross. North Eastern signals have replaced the Great Northern somersault signals which set the scene south of Doncaster. The onset of rain shortly after the author's arrival at Darlington station triggered the sudden decision to catch an express to Edinburgh for the next stage of lineside photography.

On the Down slow line north of York a 1914 Darlington-built 4–4–2 'Atlantic' class C7 No. 2170 trundles past with a slow mixed goods train. Like its sister engine this locomotive had acquired a tender from another class Q6 0–8–0, No. 2233. As the photographer received an unfriendly stare from the footplate it seemed to be the appropriate time to cycle on.

In very wet conditions on a Monday in mid-June 1941, *Empire of India* powers a Down express on the 'bridges' route to Aberdeen as it passes through Princes Street Gardens, Edinburgh. LNER A4 'Pacific' No. 4490 *Empire of India* was one of the five original Garter blue streamliners built to haul the prestigious 'Coronation' express. Each of the five had additional embellishments including an ornamental stainless steel strip along the lower edge of the valances which was repeated in line along the lower edge of the tender. Stainless steel figures and letters were fitted to the cab side and tender and, beneath the number on the cab side, the coat of arms of the country honoured by the engine name was displayed on a hand-painted plaque which gave an added splash of colour. In this case the 'Star of India' was displayed.

In atrocious June weather LNER A4 'Pacific' No. 4486 *Merlin* coasts through Edinburgh's Princes Street Gardens on the final approach to Waverley station with an Up express from Aberdeen

LNER class P2 No. 2001 *Cock o' the North*, the first of the 2–8–2 locomotives designed by Gresley for the difficult line north of Edinburgh and later rebuilt in the streamlined form, glides through Princes Street Gardens with an express from Glasgow Queen Street. Despite the incessant rain, the glistening lines of the locomotive outshine the day. The double chimney is clearly shown in this view from the foot-bridge.

Gresley's three-cylinder class V1 2–6–2T No. 2899 steams through Princes Street Gardens with a train of empty stock.

An unidentified Reid 6 ft 6 in 4–4–0, built between 1909 and 1911, works hard through Princes Street Gardens with a northbound stopping train for Dundee. This is one of the earlier 'Scott' series built by the North British Railway Company and later classified as LNER D29.

One of the first heavy freight haulage locomotives built in America to a simple design suiting our loading gauge and sent over under the terms of the 'Lease–Lend' Agreement, 2–8–0 No. 1834, is seen on initial duties in Britain hauling freight through Princes Street Gardens. The engines were painted a uniform grey with white lettering and numbering. The tenders were unique in that they had twin bogies and carried the letters USA in bold white letters. The Westinghouse brake pump was mounted at the front of the smoke box. Although photographed here in June 1941, the engines did not receive comment in the railway press until December 1942 when a brief note confirmed that some had been shipped over for general use and that people had been intrigued by the new sounding whistle. It is a paradox that, at a time when the American chime whistles were most welcome, Gresley's melodious A4 chime whistles were being removed on the pretext that they were being confused with the air-raid warning sirens. The latter sounded for a full minute at both warning and all clear!

An American 2–8–0 freight locomotive, No. 1834, awaiting the green light from the heavily hooded colour-light signals that met the stringent requirements of the blackout. The high running plates were well above the driving wheels and extended along the full length of the boiler on each side. The huge sand boxes on top of the boiler fed sand to the front of the leading coupled wheels and to the rear of the driving wheels. This, and the preceding photograph, were published in *Railways* in October 1944, over three years after being submitted, when war time restrictions were finally relaxed.

LNER A4 'Pacific' No. 4469 *Sir Ralph Wedgwood* chimes at the entrance to the tunnel mouth as it leaves Waverley with an Up express to Newcastle. Less than ten months later it was destroyed by a direct hit during an air raid on York on the night of 28/29 April 1942. The locomotive had to be scrapped as beyond repair, but its tender survived after major restoration. In January 1944 the name was resurrected and *Sir Ralph Wedgwood* name-plates replaced *Herring Gull* on No. 4466. With the wartime loss, the number of A4s was reduced to thirty-four. With the prevailing wartime restrictions this is very probably the last photograph taken of *Sir Ralph Wedgwood* before the locomotive's premature demise.

LNER A4 'Pacific' No. 4486 *Merlin*, at the head of an express to Aberdeen, awaits the departure time at the west end of Waverley station. The condition of the locomotive, after twenty-one months of war service, is exemplary.

The West Coast Main Line
LMS

After returning from Edinburgh to Darlington by rail and cycling over Stainmoor to Penrith the author continued the photographic record of the wartime railways as he continued south to follow the LMS main line from Penrith to Hest Bank.

'Jubilee' class 6P5F 4–6–0 No. 5670 *Howard of Effingham* and an unidentified 'Royal Scot' power a lengthy and unmarked express on the climb from Penrith to Shap. The abundance of wild flowers in mid-June 1941 enhanced the lineside banks.

LMS 'Coronation' class 8P No. 6225 *Duchess of Gloucester* in red and gold livery speeds bullet-like on this first stage of the climb from Penrith to Shap. Butterflies scattered out of the great profusion of flowers as the Up express to Euston roared by.

One hundred and ninety-one of the LMS class 6P5F 4–6–0s were built to replace the 'Patriots' and this locomotive, originally No. 5642, was chosen to be exhibited at Euston as part of the Silver Jubilee celebrations of 1935. It exchanged numbers with No. 5552 to become the first of the class. Many of its external fittings, including the *Silver Jubilee* name-plate, the boiler bands, steam pipes and dome, were finished in chrome for this special occasion. These embellishments are still visible on the steam pipes, on the raised numbers and letters on the cab side and tender, and on the reversing lever as *Silver Jubilee* heads south from Penrith at the start of the climb to Shap. As the 'first' of the class, it gave the latter part of its name to the whole series.

One of the original five unstreamlined 'Coronation' class 8P 'Pacifics', No. 6232 *Duchess of Montrose*, makes an easy pace with this Up express through the gently winding curves near Strickland on the climb to Shap on a hot June day in 1941.

A Stanier two-cylinder 2–6–4T No. 2596 approaching Shap summit with an early morning stopping train.

The road bridge at the north end of Shap village provided this vantage point for a late evening shot as unidentified 'Scot' class 7P climbs to the summit with an Up express. With the double summer time imposed during the wartime summers, it was light until close on midnight.

'Black Five' 4–6–0 No. 5185 with a full head of steam as it approaches Shap station and nears the summit of the climb. This was another late evening shot at the end of a very long day which took the photographer from Edinburgh to Shap.

Scout Green signal cabin controlled a minor road level crossing and the signalman made the youthful photographer welcome to spend the full day along this stretch of track. The very tall signal was visible from the far side of the moorland bank around which the track circuited and it also had a very low duplicate arm more easily seen at close quarters. A Down express hauled by 'Royal Scot' class 7P 4–6–0 No. 6157 *The Royal Artilleryman* has just passed through the level crossing as it climbs the final stretch to Shap summit.

The blue and silver lined livery of streamlined 'Pacific' No. 6223 *Princess Alice* gleams with a touch of the former splendour as the engine sweeps round the curve at Scout Green with an Up London Euston express. With the heavy demands on transport facilities made by the War Department the clean locomotive and stock were a credit to the maintenance crews.

Shortly afterwards, the second of the first five blue liveried 'Coronation' class 'Pacifics' to put in an appearance, No. 6224 *Princess Alexandra*, coasts through the level crossing with another Up London Euston express and is viewed from the south side of the cabin.

LMS modified Midland Compound 4–4–0 No. 1124 pilots an unidentified 'Royal Scot' through the
Scout Green crossing with an unmarked Up express.

'Patriot' class 6P5F 4–6–0 climbs through Scout Green with a Down mixed stock train of fitted vans and coaches.

Hughes' LMS design 2–6–0 No. 2921, built under Fowler's direction with Walschaert's valve gear, heads a Down train of mixed express freight.

'Royal Scot' class 7P 4–6–0 No. 6101 *Royal Scots Grey* working hard on a Down express at Scout Green on the climb to Shap.

The powerful exhaust of 'Jubilee' class 6P5F 4–6–0 No. 5567 *South Australia* echoes across the moor as it climbs past Scout Green with a freight train on the final stretch to Shap summit in mid-June 1941.

On the arduous climb by Scout Green this unidentified 'Jubilee' class 6P5F 4–6–0 makes steady progress with a lengthy Down express for Scotland.

LMS 'Royal Scot' class 7P 4–6–0 No. 6163 *Civil Service Rifleman* climbs to Scout Green with a Down express for Glasgow. The distant signal alongside was one of the four signals that safeguarded the minor road crossing and was operated by one of the four levers in the tiny Scout Green cabin, the crossing gates being operated manually.

An unidentified 'Black Five' takes up water at Dillicar Troughs as it speeds through with an Up express heading to the south.

An unidentified 'Coronation' class 8P streamlined 'Pacific', its maroon and gold livery somewhat tarnished, climbs towards Scout Green with a Down express for Scotland. In the warmth at the close of a very hot June day, the exhaust is invisible.

Set against the background of the Howgills maroon and gold liveried 'Coronation' class 8P 4–6–2 No. 6227 *Duchess of Devonshire* is a splendid sight as it streaks through the as yet unspoiled Lune Gorge with a Down London–Glasgow express. The second coach is one of the early twelve-wheeled kitchen cars with a clerestory roof. The destination board on the first coach was a rare occurrence in the world of wartime secrecy when written place-names were scrupulously removed. All road signposts had been lifted as part of the defence plan to confuse 'the enemy' when invasion seemed imminent.

An unidentified 'Coronation' class 8P streamlined 'Pacific' in maroon and gold livery glides smoothly round the sweeping curve by Lowgill. The old line to Sedbergh branched off the main line beyond the far reach of the curve and crossed the picturesque viaduct at Beck Foot just off this picture to the right. Only the viaduct has survived following the closure of the scenic branch line.

'Jubilee' class 6P5F 4–6–0 No. 5681 *Aboukir* with an Up express of relatively old stock speeding south towards Carnforth.

One of the original five unstreamlined 'Coronation' class 8P 'Pacifics', No. 6233 *Duchess of Sutherland*, still in immaculate condition as it heads south near Carnforth with an Up London express.

'Jubilee' class 6P5F 4–6–0 No. 5676 *Codrington* coasts downhill near Carnforth with an Up troop train. The great majority of American servicemen who subsequently arrived at the Clyde aboard one or other of the *Queens* travelled south along this line over Shap at the start of their wartime service in Europe.

Streamlined 'Coronation' class 8P 'Pacific' No. 6223 *Princess Alice* in blue and silver livery speeds through Bolton-le-Sands with an Up London Euston express.

'Black Five' 4–6–0 No. 5428 heads north near Bolton-le-Sands with a Down troop train probably destined for the Clyde.

Only two of Gresley's last design, the lightweight mixed traffic 2–6–2 locomotives class V4, were built in 1941 and the second of these, No. 3402, is seen at Doncaster station on a very dull August day in 1941. The class was discontinued as Gresley's successor, Thompson, produced large numbers of his very successful general utility engines, the B1 4–6–0s, which covered the small engine requirements.

A view of class V4 2–6–2 No. 3402 from the cab end with the Doncaster south signal-box almost obscured by the unseasonal mist. The sister engine, No. 3401, was named *Bantam Cock* and the nameless 3402 was dubbed *Bantam Hen* in consequence – one of a pair!

On the same stormy afternoon in August 1941, class A1 No. 4472 *Flying Scotsman* makes a furious start with a Down express for Newcastle. The black paint obscuring the upper glass of the railside lamp is a reminder of the national compliance with the blackout regulations which needed no emphasis after the blitz.

April 1943, and a cab side view of streamlined 'Pacific' No. 4467 *Wild Swan* shows some wartime modifications. The removal of the streamlined aerofoil skirting has revealed the whole of the motion and thereby made it more easily accessible for maintenance. The Garter blue livery has been replaced by an all-over black without any lining and the former letters 'LNER' have been replaced by 'NE' only. This photograph was taken at Grantham at the start of the return journey home from Cranwell for official leave while the author was serving in the RAFVR.

A PROPHECY
FULFILLED?

A letter from the late Mr Eric A.J. Neve printed in the December 1944 edition of *Railways* stated that if the four railway groups were merged into one national system, the initiative, enterprise and efficiency developed by the groups before the war would be stifled and killed by the dead hand of bureaucracy and that never again should we witness the epoch-making runs of the 'Silver Jubilee', 'Coronation' or Cheltenham Flyer.

On the nationalization of the railways the 'Coronation', standing in the carriage sidings at Doncaster in readiness for a post-war return, was split into small units and scattered throughout the system. Those who controlled the railway seemed totally unaware of the vast potential earning capacity that such prestigious trains would have generated even at the reduced speeds imposed by the state of the track in those immediate post-war years and the nation thus lost the most precious jewels of the LNER crown.

With prospective privatization once more on the agenda, it will be interesting to compare events with Neve's prophetic letter.

BIBLIOGRAPHY

Batty, Stephen R., *The Woodhead Route*. Weybridge, Ian Allan, 1986.
——, *This was the Woodhead Route*. Weybridge, Ian Allan, 1981.
Casserley, H.C. and Asher, L.L., *Locomotives of British Railways*. Spring Books, 1961.
Jackson, David and Russell, Owen, *The Great Central in LNER Days*, books 1 and 2. Weybridge, Ian Allan, 1983 and 1986.
Johnson, E.M., *Railways in and around the Manchester Suburbs*. Foxline Publishing, 1992.
Keeley, Raymond, *Memories of LNER Steam*. Weybridge, Ian Allan, 1980.

Railway Correspondence and Travel Society Publications: LNER Locomotives

Part 2B Tender Engines Classes B1 to B19, 1975.
Part 2A Tender Engines Classes A1 to A10, 1973.
Part 3A Tender Engines Classes C1 to C11, 1979.

Railway Magazine ,vol. LXXXV, July to December 1939.

Railways ,vol. 1, Railway World, December 1939 to June 1940.
——, vol. 2, November 1940 to December 1941.
——, vol. 3, January to December 1942.
——, vol. 4, January to December 1943.
——, vol. 5, January to December 1944.